DISCOURSE AND KNOWLEDGE – IS THE INDIVIDUAL THE BEST JUDGE OF WHAT IS RIGHT AND WRONG?

This book challenges the idea that a rational individual is the best judge of what is ethically true. It claims that individual ethical judgement is always partial. No amount of critical discussion can overcome the limitations of the individual point of view. But this does not mean that objective knowledge about morality is impossible. *Discourse and Knowledge* defends 'ethical collectivism', the view that ethical knowledge must be constructed out of the insightful but limited views which individuals bring to discourse. Ethical collectivism insists that ethical truth has to be a collective achievement.

Discourse and Knowledge moves beyond the discourse ethics of Habermas and the insights of feminist epistemologists to an ethics which takes difference seriously and yet is able to achieve a rational, impartial consensus. Janna Thompson provides a method for resolving persistent ethical disputes, and discusses the implications both for individuals and society of the adoption of an ethical method which is truly collective.

Discourse and Knowledge is a provocative and radical study which will be fascinating reading for those involved in the study of moral theory, ethics, particularly discourse ethics; those interested in the philosophy of education and to feminists concerned with knowledge and the ethics of care. Courses in social theory and on Habermas in Sociology departments will also benefit from this new approach to the debate on ethics and knowledge.

Janna Thompson is Senior Lecturer in Philosophy at La Trobe University, Melbourne, Australia. She is a well known and respected writer in the field of ethics. Her *Justice and World Order: A Philosophical Inquiry* is also published by Routledge.

DISCOURSE AND KNOWLEDGE

Defence of a collectivist ethics

Janna Thompson

London and New York

First published 1998
by Routledge
11 New Fetter Lane, London EC4P 4EE

Simultaneously published in the USA and Canada
by Routledge
29 West 35th Street, New York, NY 10001

© 1998 Janna Thompson

Typeset in Sabon by Routledge
Printed and bound in Great Britain by Clays Ltd, St. Ives PLC

British Library Cataloguing in Publication Data
A catalogue record for this book is available from the British Library

Library of Congress Cataloging in Publication Data
A catalog record for this book has been requested

ISBN 0–415–18543–2 (hb)
ISBN 0–415–18544–0 (pb)

CONTENTS

INTRODUCING ETHICAL COLLECTIVISM

This is an essay on ethical epistemology with the objective of presenting and defending a view I call ethical collectivism. Ethical collectivism is a kind of discourse ethics, a radical version of it, which insists that the correct conclusion about ethical matters is a truly collective achievement, a consensus constructed out of the diverse points of view of participants in discourse. Ethical collectivism is a thesis about the nature of ethical knowledge. It is not a view about how to make acceptable compromises on ethical issues, whether for moral or pragmatic reasons. My claim is that an agreement constructed in the right kind of discourse should not be regarded as a *modus vivendi*, as something people settle on for the sake of peace and order or because they cannot do better. A collective agreement is the closest individuals at that time and place can come to the truth of the matter (however truth is defined). It is what an individual is justified in believing is right – whatever his or her own intuitions, reasoning, conscience or experience tell her.

Ethical collectivism is a kind of discourse ethics, but it is not the same as other views which stress the importance of moral dialogue. Ethical collectivists hold that the purpose of dialogue is not merely to correct errors, exchange information and criticise theories – the usual tasks that discourse is supposed to perform. It is required for the very act of reaching a justified conclusion about ethical matters. An individual, they claim, cannot generally determine for herself what is ethically true or false, right or wrong, warranted or unwarranted – even with the critical assistance of others. She lacks the epistemological resources to make an impartial, authoritative judgment about right and wrong even after she has incorporated the ideas and criticisms of others into her moral reflections.

How ethical collectivism differs from approaches to judgment advocated by other moral philosophers (including the discourse ethics of Jürgen Habermas and Karl Otto Apel) can be clarified by a distinction between distributive and collective agreement.[1] A distributive agreement is an agreement that is reached because every rational individual, using the resources available to her (which include criticisms and information provided by

1

others), has determined for herself that a particular judgment or principle is correct. Individuals are able to agree because each using her own judgment has reached the same conclusion. A collective agreement, on the other hand, is a *constructed* consensus. It is an agreement based upon a collective consideration of the moral opinions of participants in discourse, but it is not necessarily, or usually, identical with any one of these views. It will not generally accord with any participant's own judgment about what is correct, however carefully she reasons. What I will argue is that she ought nevertheless to accept it as true, so long as she has reason to think that the procedures for reaching the result are rational, that her point of view and all other cogent views have been taken into account, and provided she has reason to believe that the conclusion agreed on, judged in the light of the standards of the procedure, is better than any other proposal that has been considered.

Ethical collectivism can also be understood as a radical criticism and rejection of 'monology'. Monologists, according to Habermas and Apel, think that a rational individual is capable of discovering for herself what is true or false. Descartes' insistence that an individual's reason, properly employed, can determine the truth about any knowable subject matter is a paradigm example of this view. Like many others, Habermas and Apel think that monology is mistaken. A knower cannot rely on her *impression* that her procedure is rational, and she cannot expect to acquire for herself all of the information, or discover for herself all of the hypotheses, on which a justified claim to knowledge depends. They argue that individuals need to belong to a community of inquiry, and to take as their objective the formulation of hypotheses which all other participants, as the consequence of rational discourse, should regard (distributively) as true.

For Habermas and Apel discourse in ethics plays the same role as discourse in science. However, their criticisms of monology, though plausible, leave a crucial vestige of the monological idea untouched. Like other philosophers they assume that an epistemological agent with an appropriate background and appropriate data, who also properly takes into account the criticisms, ideas and information provided by others, is entitled to make a knowledge claim. They assume that she has the epistemological resources to incorporate into her understanding, and pass judgment on, the contributions of all others and finally reach a conclusion about what is true. An individual can be criticised for how she does this, but the assumption is that the rational, well-informed agent has the ability and authority to make impartial judgments – judgments that others should also believe are true. Ethical collectivism rejects this remaining monological assumption, at least as far as normative ethics is concerned. It denies that an individual is entitled to make a knowledge claim, however rational she is and however conscientiously she takes into account the criticisms and views of others. Being a rational, well-informed agent is not enough to give an agent the epistemological authority to make pronouncements about what is true or false. She cannot function as a representative knower for humanity or even her community.

Ethical collectivism is a theory about the nature of ethical knowledge and how it should be obtained. It neither implies nor is implied by any particular theory about the nature of ethical value. It should not be confused with the metaphysical view that values are constructed by valuers.[2] Ethical collectivism is compatible with some versions of this thesis: those that hold that there is a rational, objective way of determining what our values should be. It is incompatible with those theories which hold that our moral evaluations are subjective or arbitrary. However, ethical collectivism is also compatible with a realist conception of the nature of value. Understood from a realist point of view, ethical collectivism claims that constructive discourse is the means we have for discovering the ethical truths of the world: that some aspects of reality can only be discovered collectively – at least by creatures like us.

Ethical collectivism is a radical epistemological theory, but the claims it makes are limited in scope. It is a theory about knowledge in normative ethics. It is not, and cannot be, a general theory about rational judgment. Ethical collectivism depends, as I will show, on individuals having the ability to make judgments for themselves about meta-ethical claims, including the statements made by ethical collectivists. I do not try to determine whether the procedure required by my theory is applicable to other subject matters, though it is possible that it is relevant to those areas of investigation, such as aesthetics, where discourse about values plays an essential role. However, ethical collectivists claim that ethical judgments are different in important respects from other kinds of judgment. In particular, they are not like empirical judgments, and ethical reasoning cannot be modelled on empirical reasoning. The nature of ethical judgments and the way they are justified motivate ethical collectivism to reject monology. No such motivation may exist in other areas of inquiry.

Ethical collectivism offers a non-standard view of what it is to be rational about ethical matters. It requires us to question what we usually take for granted about knowledge and how it is obtained. Those who first encounter it are likely to think that it is implausible, unintelligible, contradictory, or, at the very least, contrary to basic assumptions about individual integrity and moral life. I will try to show that it is none of these things. More positively, I will argue that it is a thesis supported by a plausible view about ethical judgment, and that it is superior to more familiar views about ethical rationality and judgment.

What motivates the search for an alternative account of ethical rationality is the problem of ethical disagreement. Conscientious, rational moral agents commonly disagree – not just about controversial issues, but over descriptions of particular cases, principles and their applications, and approaches to ethical theory. Disagreements are not only common; they are also persistent. Critical reflection and argument are not generally a remedy. Disagreement is often treated as the embarrassment of ethical theory. Theorists know it exists but most don't want to dwell on it. In fact, disagreement in ethics is worse than an embarrassment. It brings into question the rationality of ethical propositions and the very existence of ethical knowledge. It encourages subjectivist and decisionist views about ethical judgment. Chapters 1 and 2 are devoted to explaining why ethical theory must face this problem squarely by acknowledging how extensive disagreement is, even among those who share the same culture or background, and how deep it goes. Ethical dissonance, I will show, cannot be transcended by feats of impartiality, vanquished by proper attention to method, or argued away by discourse. Even Habermas' discourse ethics is not likely to overcome it. The problem cannot be ignored by supposing that disagreements will go away or that they can be resolved in principle. Nor can their effect be diminished by emphasising the issues on which individuals are likely to agree.

Those who happily embrace ethical differences and accept them as the inevitable result of individual difference are generally critics of the pretensions of ethical theory – its attempts to strive for impersonality or impartiality, its claims to objectivity and truth. An ethical judge, says Iris Marion Young, is always 'situated'. 'No one can adopt a point of view that is completely impersonal and dispassionate, completely separated from any particular context and commitments' (Young 1990: 103). However, these 'pretensions' are not claims that can or should be easily surrendered. The authority of ethical judgments and our ability to think of them as knowledge require ethical agents to strive for a rational consensus. Ethical collectivism provides a way of reconciling the aims of ethical theory with the recognition that agents are situated and cannot presume to be impartial. It is an attempt to rescue impartiality without denying difference.

Central to the defence of ethical collectivism as an alternative theory of ethical knowledge is a thesis about the nature of moral personality and ethical judgment. There are no fixed and standard ways of perceiving or acting in ethical situations, says Owen Flanagan (1991: 203ff.), and the moral character, and thus the moral judgments, of an individual are likely to be the result of a diversity of temperamental and environmental factors. I will argue that an investigation of the origin of moral difference suggests that an individual's moral judgment is not merely *affected* by personal factors. It is intrinsically personal. Our understanding and assessment of moral situations and moral views essentially depends upon our experiences, sympathies, antipathies, and our reflection on these in the context of our lives. The moral world is always interpreted from an individual point of view and this view cannot be transcended by critical discourse or reflection on the opinions of others. For an individual also has to interpret the criticisms and ideas of others from her own perspective.

Moral judgment, I will argue in Chapter 3, is personal. This does not mean that it is non-rational. Moral judgments can be as well-reasoned, and as well-supported by perception, theory and background knowledge as empirical judgments. It also does not mean that moral judgment is merely subjective. Those who think that ethical truth is relative to an observer are wrong. I will argue that rational agents should acknowledge that their judgments, however well-supported by experience and reflection, are partial, and that the judgments of others, even others with contrary ethical positions, can be just as germane to the truth as their own. Once we appreciate these facts about individual ethical judgment – that it is insightful but limited, rational but partial – we will find it reasonable to adopt the view of moral judgment on which ethical collectivism is based. We will regard individual judgment as making a potential contribution to the construction of a position that is truly impartial and objective.

Part I is devoted to showing that ethical collectivism is epistemologically well-motivated. Whether it can provide an intelligible and correct account of how ethical knowledge should be obtained depends upon the details of the decision-procedure it advocates: who is entitled, or required, to participate in collective decision-making, what requirements they have to satisfy, how a conclusion is constructed out of particular points of view, and what conditions it must satisfy. To explain and justify the ethical collectivist account of ethical rationality is the main business of Part II.

The decision-procedure for ethics advocated by ethical collectivism has three stages. Individuals, first of all, determine their own position on a range of related moral issues using their intuitions, understanding and reflection. These positions are then tested in critical discourse. They will be criticised, defended and amended according to standards of logic and the weight of evidence. The purpose of critical discourse is not to determine what is right or true. There is good reason to think that it cannot accomplish this objective. However, the positions which do survive critical discussion will be those which all can agree are equally cogent. Participants will finally engage in what I call a 'constructive discourse' in which they construct a conclusion out of these cogent positions. It is this conclusion which, if properly constructed, rational ethical agents are entitled and required to regard as true.

In a constructive discourse each participant will have the opportunity to make proposals about what conclusion discourse should reach given the cogent positions being considered. Each will rank the suggestions made by herself and others according to how well they accommodate what she regards as morally important. If she thinks that the proposals made so far do not adequately incorporate what she thinks is important, or that they are more favourable to the positions of others than to her own, she will put forward further proposals that better accommodate her own point of view. The acceptable proposal will be the one which achieves a 'dialogic equilibrium'. It will be the proposal that each can agree is the most satisfactory, judged in relation to all of the cogent positions presented to discourse. Each person accepts this conclusion as right not because her perception of the issues has changed. Judging from her own point of view it may still seem to her that her own position is right. She nevertheless accepts the collectively arrived at conclusion because constructive discourse has revealed that this is the position which best incorporates the ethical insights of all participants.

Ethical collectivism is supposed to provide a method for obtaining ethical knowledge and not merely a means for making acceptable compromises or finding an 'overlapping consensus'. Its advocates must therefore show that the requirements of critical and constructive discourse can be fulfilled, and that sceptical doubts about the rationality and reliability of collective reasoning can be answered. They must not only show that there is a method of constructing a conclusion which has clear and unambiguous results, but that there are good epistemological reasons for supposing that it is the only satisfactory method of doing so. They will not only have to explain how their decision-procedure for ethics works, but also define the limits of its usefulness. A defence of ethical collectivism will have to provide a plausible account of which disagreements can be resolved by construction and which cannot. In Chapter 5 I will present and defend the method of constructive discourse and also explain why I think that realists (as well as non-realists) can and should adopt it.

Ethical collectivism is opposed to accounts of ethical reasoning that come out of the Kantian and utilitarian traditions. It is also in opposition to critics of these traditions who believe that impartiality is an undesirable objective and insist that ethical judgment cannot be separated from an individual's identity, character, history, or idea of the good. Ethical collectivists allow that individual judgment is situated, but do not abandon impartiality as a requirement of ethical rationality. They are thus going to be subjected to the same criticisms as other defenders of impartiality. In addition, they have to meet the complaints of those who object to the very idea of collective ethical decision-making: who think it demeans or endangers individuals. In the concluding chapter I will be concerned with these objections. Some are easily disposed of, but others raise fundamental questions about the nature of ethics and ethical agency. I will argue that ethical collectivism provides the most satisfactory way of defending an objective which conscientious ethical agents should be reluctant to abandon. More positively, the rationality it promotes is conducive to agents adopting a respectful attitude towards others. The respect for persons it encourages is not merely a respect for the rational will that we are all supposed to share (as it is for many of those who hold a Kantian view of ethical rationality). It is an appreciation of those characteristics of an individual which enable her to develop her own moral point of view. Ethical collectivism encourages respect for differences and, along with that, a modesty about our own opinions. Its general acceptance would be desirable from an ethical, as well as a rational, point of view.

The existence of ethical collectivism owes much to my long-term interest in Jürgen Habermas' philosophy, especially his development of a discourse ethics. Habermas and his colleague Apel are not the only advocates of ethical decision-making through discourse. It has become increasingly common among feminist philosophers and those concerned with the problems posed for political ethics by multi-culturalism to recommend that individuals with different moral points of view engage in dialogue – though these proponents of discourse have different ideas about what it is and what it is supposed to accomplish.[3] This is not, however, a book about Habermas or discourse ethics as it is usually understood. I have deliberately dissociated myself from these other positions by giving my theory a name of its own.

Habermas believes that justification of our beliefs requires that we actually engage in discourse with others. The idea that justified ethical belief is what rational agents would agree to as the result of discourse is not for him a mere meta-ethical requirement (as it is for Scanlon) or an exercise of the imagination (as it is for Rawls).[4] However, neither Habermas nor any other advocate of discourse has provided a satisfactory reason for thinking that discourse is required for ethical decision-making (as I argue in Chapter 2). I was therefore led to consider whether there could be such a thing as an essentially collective ethical decision-procedure, what it would be like and would presuppose about the nature of ethical judgment. The result was ethical collectivism.

My view is that it is not only intelligible to think that ethical decisions must be made collectively. I believe that ethical collectivism is a defensible and attractive position. Ethical realists, in particular, have a lot to gain by taking it seriously. However, if I do not persuade others to accept it, I hope at least that they will find acquaintance with it stimulating.

Many individuals and collectives have contributed to the construction of the theory. My Australian colleagues John Campbell, Robert Young, Pauline Chazan, John Bigelow and Philip Pettit read and criticised various versions of this work. Others who offered useful criticisms include Susan James, Neil Thomason, Robert Sparrow, I.T. Oakley, Andrew Giles-Peters, Brian Ellis, the reviewers for Routledge, and participants in philosophy seminars at the Australian National University, Cambridge University, Manchester University, La Trobe University and University of New South Wales.

Part I

ETHICAL DISAGREEMENT:
The problem and its cause

1

CAN ETHICS BE RATIONAL? THE PROBLEM OF DISAGREEMENT

Ethical conversation is chronically conflict-ridden. Individuals, including those whose special business it is to be rational about ethical matters, find themselves at odds about a whole range of moral matters: about abortion and euthanasia, distribution of social goods, the relation of freedom and equality, the rights of individuals, the nature of family obligations, responsibilities for animals or the environment, and duties to future generations and people in other countries – to name a few issues that have been prominent in recent years. Ethical dissonance takes many forms, and disagreement can occur at any and every stage of moral judgment and reasoning. Individuals differ in their description of the moral facts, in the moral principles they hold or their justifications for them, in their interpretation and application of principles, and in their theoretical approach to moral reasoning.

Experience gives us no reason to suppose that a systematically rational approach to moral issues will bring about a convergence of opinion. On the contrary. The systems, analyses, clarifications and arguments of moral philosophers have had the effect of opening up new areas of controversy. The issue of abortion, when systematically considered by philosophers and others, has given rise to debates about the significance of stages of embryonic development, the nature and value of 'persons', the rights of women, the value of life, and the appropriateness of utilitarian and non-utilitarian approaches to moral problems. The same has happened to the theories proposed by philosophers to resolve political controversies. Rawls in *A Theory of Justice* (1973) aimed to formulate principles which all rational individuals, whatever their ideas of the good, would acknowledge as fair. What his theory has actually produced is not consensus about justice but increasingly sophisticated objections to his method or results; it has stimulated the development of rival theories of justice and a plethora of competing applications and amendments.

There is no safe refuge from moral disagreements in any tradition or cultural sanctuary. Relativism does not succeed in shutting them out. For even those who share the same ethical premises, the same creed or the same prophets often find themselves at odds about the interpretation of their

11

doctrines and their application to particular cases. Only suppression of heretical views is capable of preventing dissent from arising in a community, and as soon as this suppression is lifted, people soon discover that their ethical unanimity had more to do with power than rational persuasion. Even a retreat into radical relativism will not eliminate dissonance. An individual who insists that he or she is the measure of right can be at odds with himself about the same issues which divide individuals from each other. He may find that he holds equally weighty but conflicting moral principles, or that he is inclined to make inconsistent, but well-motivated, judgments about a particular case, or that he is attracted to incompatible moral theories.

Why ethical disagreement is a problem

The existence and persistence of ethical disagreement has often been used as a reason for rejecting ethical realism. 'The realist account of moral properties must explain why there appears to be such a great difference in apprehending or detecting their presence', says Alan Goldman (1988: 10). Disagreement about even the most basic ethical perceptions suggests that in ethics (unlike in science) 'it may not help to position the disputants in direct, causal relation to the objects of disagreement' (1988: 181). P.H. Nowell-Smith (1954: 57–8) contrasts differences in colour perception, which can reasonably be attributed to faults in the medium or in the perceiver, and disagreements about ethical properties, and concludes that if scientists disagreed in such a way about the reading of a scale or in their judgments of colour then they would be forced to decide that the property could not be real or objective.[1]

However, disagreement is not merely a problem for realists. It raises questions about the possibility of ethical rationality. One reason it does so is because of the tension it creates between what I will call the *inside* and *outside* perspectives on ethical judgment. A conscientious individual, whatever his metaphysical beliefs, is likely to regard at least some of his ethical judgments to be as self-evident or rationally well-established as his empirical judgments. They are based upon clear and distinct moral 'perceptions', backed up by justifications and theories, and tested by critical reflection. Their epistemological credentials seem impeccable. So it is reasonable for him to believe that they are as well-justified as a belief can be, and thus to think that other conscientious individuals will reach the same conclusions. Then he finds (sometimes with shock and amazement) that they do not. What's more, as a rational person, he will probably have to admit that at least some of those he disagrees with are as conscientious and rational as he is. Such considerations incline him to stand back from his convictions and see them as merely his opinions – no more rational or true than the opinions of others. But this agnosticism about the validity of moral judgments is at odds with the epistemological force of the perceptions and reasons which ground ethical convictions. The view from the outside thus leads to doubts about this epistemological basis and what claims it can support. Its effect is to undermine the strength of our convictions or the good faith with which we can hold them.

All would be well if individuals could discover, as the result of discourse and reflection, a position that all can endorse and thus regard as true. But generally such a consensus cannot be achieved, no matter how earnestly it is sought. And so ethical agents are left to waver between their own conviction of rightness and agnosticism about their own and others' ethical judgments.

The dissonance between the inside and outside view of moral judgments accounts for a familiar inconsistency in common views about morality. When people are engaged in thinking about moral issues that really matter to them, they are naturally inclined to take the inside view. They believe that what they think is right *is* right, especially when they have good reasons to back up their judgments. When they are thinking in a less engaged way about moral matters (as in a class on moral philosophy), they find it equally natural to take the outside view – to see their moral judgment as just one personal opinion among others. A good teacher of moral philosophy can often persuade students that the outside view does not accord with the role that moral judgment plays in their lives. However, the fact that serious moral agents do not think that the results of their reasoning are mere personal opinions does not establish that the view from the inside is right, and it does not solve the problem which makes the outside view attractive.

If the outside view is right, then it is natural to suppose that there must be something wrong with the view from the inside. The dissonance between the inside and outside perspectives thus opens the door to subjectivism, scepticism or nihilism. A subjectivist claims that moral judgments are nothing more than an expression of individual taste, the result of upbringing, cultural attitudes or personal idiosyncrasy. Moral agents, for all their ratiocination, can make no claim to objectivity, according to the subjectivist. If the inside view encourages us to have this pretension, then it is the source of illusion. A sceptic about knowledge argues that ethical reasoning, however conscientious, cannot be relied upon to give us anything that we can call an ethical truth or even a justified ethical belief. The inside view is a total illusion. The nihilist says that there is no such thing as ethics, as this is usually conceived, or that what purports to be ethics is really a contest of power. All of these positions can be regarded as forms that scepticism about ethical rationality can take. In ethics scepticism is not merely a form of philosophical play. The problems which give rise to doubts about moral rationality and moral judgment are everyone's problems. They affect our perceptions of ethical matters, undermine confidence in moral judgment, and encourage cynicism about the true motivations of moral agents.

The problem of the relation between inside and outside views of ethical judgment is a difficulty for each agent in relation to his own moral convictions and his search for truth. Another reason why disagreement leads to doubts about ethical rationality is that it seems to undermine the public, or inter-personal, authority which moral judgment is supposed to possess. It raises doubts about the objectivity of ethics. Moral philosophers commonly insist that moral judgments or generalisations are by nature propositions on which all rational individuals should agree. Kant expresses this requirement in his famous formula: 'Act according to the maxim that you can will without contradiction to be a universal law of mankind'. The universalisability of the moral law, as Kant understands it, is not merely the formal requirement that whatever I deem to be right or wrong I must hold to be right or wrong for anyone else who finds himself in the same circumstances. Ethical agents must strive not just for consistency but also for objectivity. Implicit in Kant's formula is the idea that moral principles are supposed to apply to and be applied by everyone. Moral rationality thus requires agents to propound principles which all rational individuals can and should endorse. To legislate for humankind an individual must transcend his own interests and empirical circumstances and speak as the possessor of a rational will, the identity he shares with all other individuals.

Contemporary philosophers have largely abandoned Kant's metaphysics and the idea that non-contradiction is an adequate test of a moral principle. However, most of them either retain in some other form his idea of what universalisability means or regard it as a necessary, if not sufficient, condition of ethical rationality. Habermas converts Kant's 'monological' approach into the requirement that what is right is the consensus rational moral agents would reach in a universal discourse under ideal conditions. Rawls and his followers use the idea of a hypothetical contract among rational agents to elucidate what moral rationality requires. Richard Brandt (1959: 21) divides Kant's requirement into two tests for ethical principles, both of which he thinks are intuitively obvious. Consistency requires that we treat like cases alike. Generality requires that moral judgments and maxims be acceptable to all. Ethics is a subject matter which presupposes a common rationality, he says, and we cannot regard a judgment to be rational if it favours some individuals over others or if it depends upon considerations that do not move others. Kurt Baier (1958: 195) argues for similar reasons that the moral point of view by its nature requires acting on principles which are universally binding. Joel Kupperman (1983: 35) thinks that it is inherent in moral judgments that they be shared: 'that others, from their perspective should see roughly what one sees from one's own perspective'. Scanlon (1982: 110) thinks that moral motivation, our conviction of rightness, depends upon the possibility of making judgments according to a system of rules which 'no one could reasonably reject as a basis for informed, unforced general agreement'.

However, the agreement required is often not forthcoming. So if consensus is essential to how ethics is defined, or what ethical truth means, or to the authority that ethical propositions can claim, then the existence of disagreement is not a mere inconvenience or embarrassment, but something that threatens the subject matter of ethics itself.

Dealing with dissonance: the strategy of containment

The *fact* that people disagree about moral matters does not prove that there is no right answer to ethical questions or that consensus is not possible. John Pollock thinks that

> it could well be the case that people differ in their moral judgments just because moral judgments are hard to make. They might have the rational equipment needed to resolve most moral disagreements but fail to do so because such resolution is difficult.
>
> (Pollock 1985: 522)

Nicholas Sturgeon (1984: 49) thinks that a lot of our moral disagreements may be the result of non-moral influences, like that of religious belief, or the result of distorting factors like personal interest or social ideology. Derek Parfit (1984: 454) points out that non-religious ethics is at a very early stage and suggests that we aren't in a position to predict whether agreement will eventually be reached, and that it is not irrational to think that it will.

Alternatively, defenders of ethical rationality may concede that disagreement is sometimes irresolvable, but argue that this does not require us to call into question the rationality or objectivity of moral judgment. Susan Wolf suggests that ' . . . the question of what is right in some cases lacks a unique and determinate answer' (1992: 102) but argues that value pluralism does not have to lead to subjectivism or scepticism. Judith DeCew (1990), Amy Gutmann (1993) and Stuart Hampshire (1983) allow that ethical agreement is not always possible, especially among people of different cultures and social backgrounds, but that this does not mean that scepticism, or even relativism, is vindicated.

The first strategy for dealing with moral dissonance attempts to transcend it, or show that transcendence is possible 'in principle'; the second admits the existence of untranscendable moral conflict but argues that it does not threaten the authority, objectivity or rationality of ethics. This strategy seeks to contain or render harmless ethical dissonance. Let us consider each strategy in more detail, starting with the second.

Susan Wolf argues that agents may have to acknowledge in some cases that the contrary views of others are no less rational and well supported than their own and that there is no over-arching principle or value which can decide the issue. She suggests that some of the conflicting positions taken in the abortion debate could be examples of this kind of disagreement. Admitting the possibility of value conflict need not lead to subjectivism – the

15

view that our ethical judgments are merely the expression of brute or unfounded psychological attitudes. Rational agents should simply acknowledge, according to Wolf, that there is no right answer in these cases about what one morally ought to do. Her position invites us to look at moral disputes as being similar to empirical cases where commonly used criteria do not provide a unique or definite answer to some questions.[2]

Wolf is in effect allowing that the outside perspective on ethical judgment is sometimes the right view to take. She says that we should sometimes adopt an 'agnostic' view towards our own judgments in relation to the judgments of others. One of the problems with this way of dealing with dissonance is that it does not fit the facts of ethical debate. The empirical disagreements which Wolf refers to generally come to an end once it is pointed out that the disputants are using different criteria for judgment or that existing criteria are not sufficient to determine what judgment should be made. Disputes about ethical matters are not generally treated in this way. Doubts about criteria often lead instead to a different level of ethical disagreement: from arguments about abortion (for example) to arguments about what should count as a person or what rights persons have. Moreover, disputes about ethical matters cannot generally be confined to a single issue or pinned down to the use of a particular term. Someone who conscientiously reasons about abortion or other controversial matters is likely to believe, not only that his view is right, but that it follows from, or is no less certain than, other principles or values that he holds. It would be difficult for him to take the 'agnostic' point of view which rationality seems to require – at least without this affecting his attitude towards other judgments and values. Wolf, herself seems to demonstrate the difficulty of taking seriously the pluralist view of morality by admitting that issues like abortion 'are ones which, after much reflection, I find myself thinking have a right answer after all' (Wolf 1992: 798).

Wolf identifies a second level of pluralism which seems to take into account the fact that disagreements can be global as well as local, that people may disagree in their moral codes or outlooks, as well as in their views about particular issues. If global disagreements are irresolvable, she says, then relativism of a certain kind is true, but this does not lead to scepticism about moral rationality. For if these different moral codes can be equally well-supported by arguments and reasons, then it is not irrational for individuals to adhere to their particular code and regard it as binding on them. A member of the pacifist Amish sect can appreciate the position of someone who thinks that violence is sometimes justified, and the other can appreciate the Amish position; each can acknowledge that the other's position is rational in its own terms, and yet each can regard himself as justified in believing and following his own code.[3] What Wolf is trying to show is that a person can (sometimes) accept the outside perspective on his judgments without undermining his ethical convictions or succumbing to subjectivism.

If the member of the Amish community believes in non-violence because he thinks this is the command of God, and the other individual has a non-religious justification for his ethical beliefs, then it is not difficult to understand how each agent can recognise that the other has his own good reasons for what he believes, and yet remain firmly committed to his own belief. What divides these agents is not merely a difference of judgment or principle but a different conception of rational justification. They do not belong to the same ethical discourse or community of inquiry, and thus what one believes and argues has no bearing on the beliefs of the other (just as beliefs in the supernatural have no relevance to science). No one needs to be epistemologically perturbed about the fact that people with different ideas about rational justification often end up with different beliefs.[4]

What is disturbing about many cases of ethical disagreement is that they take place among people who accept the same general criteria of rationality – among people who can discuss and argue with each other, and think that being rational requires taking each other's position into account, but nevertheless end up with different views on a whole range of issues. It is disturbing because each agent, having reasoned well and taken all relevant considerations into account, has reason to believe he is right. If other agents, whom he has to acknowledge are rational in the same sense that he is, think differently then how can he retain confidence in his own convictions? Agnosticism in such cases is no solution, but rather a triumph for scepticism. Nor is it a solution to ignore the fact of disagreement and commit yourself to your own beliefs. If the outside perspective, which tells you that your view is no more rational than the views of others, is right, then it cannot be ignored. For it means that your commitment cannot be justified, that it is a matter of faith or assertion. Subjectivism has, after all, won the day. In short, Wolf's way of dealing with dissonance does not resolve the tension between the inside and outside perspectives on ethical judgment. She does not adequately defend the objectivity, authority and rationality of ethical judgment.

Wolf says that her defence of pluralism depends on the assumption that conflicts between rational individuals are not total. Individuals may differ in their moral opinions or even their moral systems, but they share sufficient common ground for them to agree that some moral judgments and systems are simply wrong. They can determine in common the parameters of moral debate.

> Second level pluralism and the relativism that is based on it, then, are not versions of the . . . view that anything you really believe is right is right for you or that anything a society endorses is right for that society's members.
>
> (Wolf 1992: 797)

17

Another way of understanding her strategy is to think of it as a way of discounting disagreement. What rational individuals agree on, she seems to be saying, is far more basic and extensive than are their disagreements. Once we recognise this, then dissonance, even irresolvable disagreements, seems less threatening to ethics as a rational enterprise.

This defence of ethical rationality is elaborated by others who adopt the containment strategy for dealing with ethical dissonance. Amy Gutmann acknowledges that there may be irresolvable cultural differences about some moral matters, but that more significant (at least as far as political ethics is concerned) are the fundamental matters on which individuals agree.

> No culture or political community with which we are familiar gives its members good reasons for rejecting principles or practices that protect innocent people from being enslaved, tortured, murdered and malnourished, imprisoned, rendered homeless or subject to abnormal physical pain and sickness.
>
> (Gutmann 1993: 189)

DeCew distinguishes between two kinds of relativism: one which admits the existence of *some* irresolvable ethical disagreement and a more radical version which claims that there is no unique rational method in ethics. As long as there are some moral norms or values or solutions which can be justified cross-culturally (and DeCew clearly thinks there are), then radical relativism is false, and we do not have to succumb to the scepticism about ethics which it encourages (DeCew 1990: 35ff.).[5]

However, the difference between the forms of relativism which DeCew identifies is one of degree and not kind, and scepticism too can be a matter of more or less. Our commonalities do not preserve us from the suspicion that opinions concerning controversial issues are merely subjective, and the more extensive or basic the conflict, the more open to doubt is the rationality and objectivity of ethical judgment. The problem is not merely that the consensual core may not be extensive enough to rescue ethics from the sceptics, but that divergence underlies even the matters on which we agree. Consensus about whether an action or situation is bad or good does not mean that people agree in their generalisations or their justifications. Behind every moral agreement lurks potential for dissonance, awaiting its opportunity to emerge. Disputes are likely to begin as soon as people are forced to reflect on the reasons for their judgments, as soon as they advance a general rule, or when they start appealing to the 'obvious' cases in order to defend judgments about more controversial matters.

Every minimally rational ethical agent (let us assume) would condemn a parent who tortures his child. This condemnation can be made from a number of perspectives – points of view which are likely to affect the way in which people generalise from this particular case or what they compare it with. One person thinks that a parent who tortures his child deserves condemnation because he is causing great physical and mental suffering, another because the child is an innocent being. Another thinks of the action as wrong, above all, because it is a serious violation of the parental duty of care. Another thinks of it as a case of harming a *human being* – someone whose suffering ought to have a special meaning for us (Gaita 1991: 117–20). These differences in the way the case is perceived lead people in different ethical directions when they use it as a reference point for arguing about other matters. The person who thinks that what is especially wrong is the distress and pain that the child suffers, or who thinks that the innocence of the child has a special moral relevance will be predisposed to think that the torture of animals should be condemned for similar reasons. Those who stress the relation of the child to the parent or the child's status as a human being are not likely to think that the torture of an animal is a comparable wrong. Similarly, differences of opinion lie behind the (almost) universal condemnation of slavery and violence. Some may condemn slavery or violence because of the physical and mental harm they do to individuals; others place more emphasis on the effect of slavery on relations between individuals or the destruction of trust which violence entails. People can agree that slavery or violence is wrong, and yet disagree about what this wrong is: whether it is a violation of a human right or simply an injury to an individual's well-being; about what constitutes an injury or what rights individuals have, and what having them means.

Disputants can agree that slavery or violence is wrong and yet disagree about what slavery or violence *is*. Some define 'slavery' as the ownership of one human being by another; some use the term to describe other relationships of power and subordination. For some people 'violence' is simply physical assault. Others think that psychological torment or institutional exercises of power count as violent. These differences are not merely semantic; nor can they be regarded simply as disputes about matters of fact. They seem to be bound up with different conceptions of what is wrong with violence or slavery and how these wrongs are related to other wrongs, with different moral views about power, how it is exercised and its effects on people, and with different ideals concerning personal and social relationships.

People who disagree about why torture, slavery or violence is wrong, or about what the terms mean, still have a common ground. They not only make the same judgments about right and wrong in many cases; they are also likely to have ideas about ethical rationality which are similar enough so that they can fruitfully argue with each other. But this is not enough of a commonality to establish that sceptics about ethical rationality are wrong. The containment strategy does not work. First of all, because it does not succeed in quarantining controversy or showing that subjectivism is wrong. And second, because it does not do justice to our accomplishments and aims as rational ethical agents: to the systematic way in which our ethical beliefs, controversial and not-so-controversial, are related, and to our conviction that we should strive, through reflection and argument, to resolve our disagreements and reach conclusions that are rational and right. Those who argue that disagreement can be transcended are attempting to defend this common view of what ethical discourse should accomplish.

Transcendence and the idea of the ideal agent

Theorists who aim for transcendence think that ethical disagreement can be resolved, if not in fact, then *in principle*. To say that we can do something 'in principle' could mean that we possess the capacities required to accomplish it: that if we are persistent and rational in our pursuit of truth we will eventually resolve our conflicts, or at least make progress in doing so. This is what Parfit means when he says that it is reasonable to hope that systematic ethical inquiry will eventually lead to consensus. The idea that we can make progress in ethical reasoning has empirical support. Only a few generations ago it was common for even well-educated people to approve of racial segregation and discriminatory treatment of minority racial groups – practices which are now widely condemned as racist. It would probably be wrong to regard the rejection of these practices as merely a change of fashion or the result of political pressure (though social changes undoubtedly made people more receptive to anti-discrimination arguments). A reasonable account of what happened is that thoughtful individuals, when encouraged to reflect on the practices of their society, came to believe that discrimination depended on false empirical ideas about race, or on insensitivity to the needs and points of view of others, or on an inadequate view about justice, or a self-interested unwillingness to perceive injustice. An evolution of moral opinion has clearly taken place. The question is whether this example can serve as a model for how controversial ethical issues can be resolved.

One problem is that many ethical disagreements do not seem to be caused by any failing on the part of disputants or by a lack of information or appreciation. Many of those who disagree about abortion, capital punishment, justice, or the rights of animals seem to have all of the empirical information they need (though they have different ideas about its relevance). They seem to be equally able to appreciate the consequences of their proposals and the feelings of those concerned; and they seem equally capable of arguing for their views and appreciating the arguments of others. It does not seem possible (in a non-question-begging way) to point to any failing or lack, the remedy of which would result in rational consensus. The second difficulty is that ethical progress, as we know it, has a tendency to generate *disagreement*. While resolving some issues it turns the spotlight of ethical debate onto others. Most of us now agree that individuals are of equal worth. We do not agree about what this means or what its implications should be for social policy or on what constitutes unjust discrimination. There is no way of ruling out the possibility that these ethical issues can be resolved, but our experience of ethical controversy gives us reason to think that Parfit's hope is unrealistic. Ethical dissonance seems to be a permanent fixture of our ethical lives.

However, to say that something is resolvable in principle does not need to imply that we are actually capable of resolving it. We could, after all, be so flawed in our ability to reason, so captivated by our prejudices, so incapable of impartiality, or so imperfectly informed that we will never reason properly concerning ethical matters. If this is our problem, then failure to agree does not mean that there are no right answers to ethical questions. 'The idea', says Thomas Nagel, 'is that in [many cases of disagreement] there is a common reason in which both parties share, but from which they get different results because they cannot, being limited creatures, be expected to exercise it perfectly' (Nagel 1987: 234). This suggests that a being who did not have our limitations would be capable of getting things right. R.M. Hare imagines that ethical judging is done by an archangel who is not hindered by our imperfections. To the extent that we can judge like an archangel, he says, we judge correctly (Hare 1981: 44–6). Of course, it is unlikely that we will ever succeed, or know that we have done so.

Why should we take Hare's supernatural agent as our earthly ideal? If it is to be of any help in countering subjectivism and scepticism, an interpretation of 'resolvable in principle' requires more than the supposition that there is an answer to our ethical questions. God (if there is such a being) knows all ethical truths (if there are such things), but a reference to what God knows does not make sense of the claim that our ethical conflicts are resolvable. To say that *we* can resolve ethical disagreement means that we do so in some possible world – a world in which we do not suffer from our existing shortcomings. This presupposes that these more fortunate beings are recognisable as 'us'. For otherwise our epistemological doubts and difficulties will not be dealt with; otherwise scepticism about ethical rationality will not be refuted. So someone who claims that ethical disagreements are resolvable in principle must either establish that there is a rational procedure which, if we could follow it better than we ever do, would give us the right answers; or that questions of right could be resolved by beings who are like us except for lacking the limitations which prevent us from reasoning well.

This suggests that there are two ways to make sense of the claim that ethical agreement is possible in principle. The first is to use our knowledge of what makes some ethical judgments better than others to specify the properties an ideal ethical agent must have in order to make correct judgments. This is the strategy used by Roderick Firth (1952), Richard Brandt (1979), John Rawls (1973), David A.J. Richards (1971) and Stephen Darwall (1983). The second is to provide an ethical decision-procedure – the method or rules which are capable of giving us the right answer to ethical questions.

This is the aim of Rawls in his early 'Outline of a decision procedure for ethics' (1951), Norman Daniels (1979), Hare (1963) and others who adopt the utilitarian approach to moral decision-making. These ways of showing how to reach agreement in principle are not mutually exclusive. An account of ideal agency is also likely to say or presuppose something about how individuals ought to reason, and ethical decision-procedures generally require agents to have particular characteristics and abilities. Nevertheless, these strategies are sufficiently different to require separate discussion.

Our 'common reason' provides us with criteria for making judgments about the performance of ethical judges. We can fail to judge well because of prejudice, insensitivity, self-interest, lack of knowledge, or because of bad logic. So why not suppose that the ideal ethical judge is simply an agent who suffers from none of these disabilities, or is able to divest himself of them? If ethical disagreement can be transcended then it seems that such a being will do so. Roderick Firth defines ethical truth in terms of the responses of an all-knowing, dispassionate and disinterested ideal observer. Having these qualities not only ensures that the observer knows whatever he needs to know in any ethical situation, but that he is not influenced by his own interests, passions or relationships. He cannot be anything else but impartial and objective (Firth 1952: 333ff.). Brandt thinks that the right moral judgments will be made according to the moral code chosen by an individual who has undergone a thorough and effective course of 'cognitive psychotherapy' (Brandt 1979: 306).[6] This agent has not only examined and criticised the desires and motivations which influence moral judgment – rejecting those which are prejudiced, or the result of ignorance or an unfortunate upbringing. He has also taken steps to replace them with desires and aversions which are completely rational: those which survive critical examination in the light of all relevant information about their source, nature and effects. Firth's agent, like Hare's archangel, is ideal by nature; Brandt's agent is supposed to achieve ideal rationality by methods which are themselves rational.

If ethical agents can ever come to an agreement about what is right, then it seems that the ideal agents imagined by Firth and Brandt should be able to do so. Both of them think that ideal agents would agree, but are willing to allow that relativism could turn out to be true: ideal observers and fully rational agents may respond differently to moral situations and advocate different moral codes. Nevertheless, the qualities of ideal agents, their lack of lacks, are supposed, at least, to ensure that they will achieve whatever agreement there is to be had. This should mean that they will at least be able to agree on what is right within the framework of the assumptions of their tradition or community.

Behind Firth and Brandt's imaginings is the assumption that agents become more rational, and thus more likely to agree in their judgments, as they become more dispassionate, impersonal or fully informed. Partiality or the failure to appreciate fully all possible points of view stands in the way of rational consensus. This assumption is problematic. If being impersonal and dispassionate or having full information means merely that the agents are unprejudiced, open minded, and free from the influence of self-interest, according to our ordinary understanding of what this means, then ideal agency theory does not show how disagreements are resolvable in principle. If being an ideal agent requires a more drastic attack on personality or point of view, then ideal agency theory threatens the very possibility of moral judgment.

Suppose that I believe that women should be able to have abortions if they want them. Becoming fully informed about my judgment, according to Brandt, would require complete understanding of what motivates it. He is right to think that what I discover could show me that my opinion is not rationally grounded. If I find that I support abortion because I am reacting to the beliefs of my conservative parents, then my stance is undermined by cognitive psychotherapy. I will either have to change my view or find some better reason for holding it. On the other hand, if I discover that my view is motivated by an empathy for women who are forced to go through unwanted pregnancies, an identification which results from my particular experiences and outlook, then it is not obvious that cognitive psychotherapy could or should persuade me that I am being irrational. In fact, a reflection on my motivations may only confirm me in my opinion that my judgment is well-founded.

Brandt's belief that cognitive psychotherapy can resolve moral disputes is based upon the reasonable idea that moral judgments can go wrong, not merely because individuals sometimes reason badly, but because their capacity to perceive, judge and reason can itself be perverted by personal characteristics or habits of thought. People can be prejudiced, insensitive, blind to certain considerations or over-sensitive to others. The problem for any programme of cognitive psychotherapy is how we should distinguish between features of personality which make ethical judgment perverse and those which merely make judgments different. Ethical agents, faced with disagreement, have a natural tendency to think that those who judge differently *must* be perverse. Such accusations are question-begging unless there are independent grounds for them. Experience gives us good reason to suspect that if cognitive psychotherapy removes merely those positions which are prejudiced, ignorant or insensitive, according to our ordinary understanding of these failings, it will leave many disagreements still standing. If it is expected to do more, it will itself be vulnerable to the accusation of partiality.

Brandt himself has no intention of misusing cognitive psychotherapy in this way. He merely wants to ensure that agents are fully informed, not only about the genesis of their own views, but also about the situation of others (1979: 206). This is likely to include the ethical opinions of these others.

However, there is reason to suspect that he is trying to get more from cognitive psychotherapy than it can deliver. If being fully informed about the situation of others means that we should understand, appreciate and take into account their needs, interests and moral views, then this requirement of cognitive psychotherapy is reasonable, but is not likely to result in agreement. For I will be evaluating their attitudes and opinions from my own perspective, and even when dialogue with others causes me to re-think my position, my judgment will be informed by my particular attitudes and sympathies. If becoming vividly aware of the point of view of another person means that I must evaluate it exactly like he does and not judge it from my own perspective, then cognitive psychotherapy seems to be imposing an unreasonable requirement on me. The problem is not just how I can acquire vivid awareness, so understood, but why I should acquire it and whether it would do me any good if I did. If my perspective is a reasonable one – not based on error or misinformation – then why shouldn't I use it as a basis for judgment? If I am not supposed to judge from my perspective (or any particular perspective), then how can I rationally reach a conclusion?[7] If the differences which produce dissonance are reproduced within my psyche, then how can I make a non-arbitrary decision about what is right? Brandt can't assume that the agent will be able to make a judgment under the conditions imposed by cognitive psychotherapy. Not without more information about how this is possible.

The defects of Firth's ideal observer theory are even more obvious. He presupposes rather than proves that there is a neutral or impersonal point of view, a perspective that transcends all perspectives. The problem is not simply that it's impossible for us to know what decisions an impersonal, dispassionate observer would reach. We have no reason for believing that such an agent could manage to reach a moral conclusion at all. We have no reason to think that there *is* an impersonal, impartial point of view. However, if an impersonal point of view turns out to be no view at all, then eliminating the personal also eliminates the very possibility of ethical judgment.

A more down to earth, and therefore more promising, way of creating an ideal agent is to employ Rawls' veil of ignorance to make impartial ethical reasoners out of ordinary agents. Stephen Darwall and David A.J. Richards think that this device, which Rawls uses for reasoning about justice, can be used more generally in ethics to bring about rational agreement concerning principles, or at least show how this is possible. They assume that irrationality and disagreement have the same cause: the influence exerted by particular interests and values. So if rational agents are required to make choices of principle without knowledge of their sex, race, religion, idea of the good, or any other facts about themselves, then all the factors responsible for bias, and therefore disagreement, will be eliminated.[8] The veil of ignorance is supposed to bring about what Nagel calls the highest order of impartiality which 'takes us outside ourselves to a standpoint that is independent of who we are' (Nagel 1987: 16).[9]

The problem is that a veil of ignorance which merely separates us from knowledge about ourselves is not likely to achieve Nagel's ideal. It is also likely to fail to bring about a moral consensus. For even if individuals are prevented from appealing to personal interests or values this will not stop them from being influenced in their judgments by their character and personal predilections. As long as they remain the individuals they are, they will, presumably, have sympathies, aversions and dispositions which will affect the way they respond, think and judge, even from behind a veil of ignorance.

Darwall takes this consideration to mean that the veil of ignorance must operate at a deeper psychological level. To become truly independent of who they are, individuals must be divested of the influences, conscious or unconscious, which derive from their particular standpoint and personality. 'This means that there is in effect only one chooser behind the veil: an arbitrary rational agent' (Darwall 1983: 231). His critic, Iris Marion Young, wonders how an agent who has been stripped of all his interests and sympathies is able to make a moral judgment at all (Young 1990: 103). This is a reasonable complaint. Darwall, like Firth, cannot simply assume that an agent with no particular dispositions, sympathies, attitudes and ways of perceiving will manage to respond morally to situations, or reach any conclusions about them. He also cannot assume that the responses of beings who are so different from us have any relevance to our epistemological situation. This means that he has not provided an adequate interpretation of what it means to reach agreement in principle.

Ideal agency theories face a common predicament. If, in specifying the qualities of the ideal agent, they hold to a commonsense conception of what it is to judge in an unbiased way, then why should we believe that all factors which lead to disagreement will be eliminated? Experience of ethical disagreement suggests that we are still likely to end up with a plurality of ethical opinions. On the other hand, if they try to eliminate all sources of difference they are in danger of ending up with no ethical judgments at all, or no judgments that are relevant to our epistemological situation. As long as there are doubts about the possibility of higher-level impartiality, ideal agency theory cannot show that disagreements are resolvable in principle. What is needed in order to escape this predicament is supposed to be supplied by the second way of making sense of 'resolvable in principle': a decision-procedure which gives us reason to believe that if ethical agents could reason correctly, they would converge on the same conclusion.

A decision-procedure for ethics?

Method need not guarantee that a convergence in beliefs will ever occur. Consider the fable of the blind men who encounter what they are told is an elephant. Having come into contact with a different part of the beast, each of them reaches a different conclusion about what is there. The one who touches the tail believes that an elephant is a brush; the one who stumbles against the leg believes it is a pillar, and so on. There are several possible morals to this story. One is merely a warning about jumping to conclusions. We can also take it as a lesson about human limitations. The blind men may never reach an agreement, however well-motivated they are: because they do not have enough time, because they do not hit upon any hypothesis capable of accounting for their disparate perceptions, or because they never acquire sufficient evidence to decide which of several hypotheses is correct. They might never completely overcome their preconceptions and biases. Determining the truth of the matter may simply be beyond their capacity. The existence of a method for resolving such disputes warrants a belief that they can make progress towards a correct conclusion: that they can in principle, if not in practice, reach a rational consensus about what is there.

Let us suppose that they proceed as follows (though there is not necessarily just one way of proceeding). Each observes what the others have identified as a pillar, a brush, etc. and confirms that it *does* feel like these things. Since the identifications are incompatible, they recognise that they can't all be right, and so they concentrate on describing more exactly what it is that made it seem like a pillar or a brush. ('This feels rough and round'; 'this feels stringy'.) All observe what the others have observed and confirm or criticise these more basic descriptions. They will then propose various hypotheses which make sense of all the observations and test these hypotheses by further observations (and sometimes by revising their descriptions). If they have enough time and patience; if they have sufficient evidence and ingenuity, it is reasonable to believe that they will eventually arrive at a justified conclusion about what is really there: a Big Picture which is the result of each individual being forced by the procedure to revise his perceptions and theories so that they become observations and theories acceptable to all.

Rawls in his 1951 'Outline of a decision procedure for ethics' conscientiously models ethical decision-making on inductive method.[10] He first defines a class of competent moral judges. These are individuals of normal intelligence who are morally motivated, knowledgeable about the cases they are judging and possess 'a sympathetic knowledge of human interests' (1951: 179). He then specifies the circumstances in which they can be relied on to make 'considered moral judgments' about particular cases. They must be capable of taking a detached view: they must not be subject to threats and their own interests must not be at stake. From the class of considered judgments of competent judges, principles are 'explicated' which seem most satisfactorily to embody what is essential to the particular judgments. The reasonableness of a principle, says Rawls, depends on whether in other, more difficult cases it can 'yield a result which, after criticism and discussion, seems to be acceptable to all, or nearly all, competent judges, and to conform to their intuitive notion of a reasonable decision' (1951: 188). Ethical method, in other words, uses ethical perceptions and the judgments that arise from them as the basis for general hypotheses which are then tested by further judgments about particular cases, and judgments about particular cases are themselves open to revision in the light of well-confirmed hypotheses.

Judges, like the blind men of the fable, may begin by disagreeing about many matters. The method forces them to concentrate on what their moral 'perceptions' actually tell them; (Rawls says that they are supposed to judge a case without making use of preconceived ideas about general principles), and to ensure that the principles they finally affirm are supported by the 'evidence'. Having agreed on principles, Rawls assumes that they should be able to reach agreement about the more difficult cases to which the principles can be applied – thus resolving the disagreements which occur when such cases are first encountered. He is not assuming that this will always be possible. In ethics as in science there may be matters on which existing principles are not capable of pronouncing, and sometimes our personal or human limitations may prevent us from reaching the right result. However, the method is supposed to ensure that agreement is generally possible and to tell us how we can achieve it, or at least make progress towards it.

Nevertheless, there is a notable difference between empirical method and moral method, as Rawls conceives it – a difference which brings into doubt his view about what method can accomplish, even in principle. Ethical decision-making requires that judges have a competency which empirical reasoning does not require – the ability to appreciate in a sympathetic way the interests of people whose case they are judging. Appreciation is not merely a matter of understanding others, something that a competent psychologist will also want to do. Sympathetic appreciation is what enables the competent judge to make moral evaluations, and it also directs his valuing.

In the case of empirical method we reasonably assume that agents will eventually reach an agreement about what evidence is relevant and how data should be described and assessed (or at least agreement can be expected among those who share the same theoretical framework). We can make no such assumption in ethics. It is all too likely that the sympathetic appreciation of judges will lead them to evaluate cases differently and/or to explicate their judgments in contrary ways. Actual disagreements among people who count as competent judges suggest that this is what often happens. If method is to achieve its end then it must provide us with criteria or procedures to direct our sympathies.

Rawls does provide us with some directions about how we should employ our sympathetic appreciation. A competent judge is supposed to use his own experiences and imagination to appreciate the interests of others as if they were his own, bestowing 'upon the appraisal of each the same care which he would give to it if that interest were his own' (1951: 179). Sympathetic appreciation itself embodies a moral prescription: that everyone's interests ought to be respected equally. This means that Rawls' judges are not entirely free from preconceived ethical opinions – a worry for those who want to know how this moral assumption should itself be justified. Rawls might defend himself by claiming that there is no way of providing a method for ethics without making ethical assumptions. Nevertheless, it is a cause for concern that the claim that individuals should be equally respected has been regarded in the history of ethics as something that requires argument. I will say more about this matter in Chapter 4.

Assuming that individuals deserve equal consideration, we still have to know what it means to regard the interests of others as being as important as our own. There are well-known differences of opinion about how we should do this (and also differences of opinion about who or what counts as an other or a morally significant interest). Hare thinks it means that we should imagine ourselves in the place of others with the interests that they have and then weigh these interests in relation to each other to determine which course of action would maximise their satisfaction (Hare 1963: 123). Others think that this utilitarian way of treating interests is not an appropriate way of respecting others. In any case, experience tells us that competent judges can heed Rawls' requirement and yet come up with different moral observations. If Rawls' method is to resolve disagreements among competent judges then it must either be more specific about how interests are to be treated or it must provide some further criteria for judging the observations, explications or generalisations of competent judges.

Being more specific about how interests should be treated means taking sides in the debates which rage among consequentialists of various kinds and deontologists of various kinds. This is itself a problem. If there are competent judges who are consequentialists and others who are not, then what justifies a stipulation that a particular procedure should be adopted? Without a decisive argument for preferring one party in the disputes over others, a decision is going to seem arbitrary and unacceptable to many agents who otherwise count as competent judges. So far ethical theory has produced no generally accepted reasons for preferring one way of assessing interests over others. This too is a perennial subject of ethical disagreement.

Even if we do decide on a particular method for assessing interests, it is not likely that the problem of disagreement among competent judges will go away. Let us suppose that all competent judges adopt Hare's utilitarian conception of how interests should be assessed. Could we expect most competent judges to make the same judgments about individual cases? Could we at least suppose that archangels, who are aware of all interests and can foresee all the consequences of courses of actions, would do so? The answer is not likely to be 'yes'. For utilitarians have plenty of things to argue about: what counts as an interest; how interests (which take many different forms and are related to each other and the self in different ways) should be ranked; whether and how the interests of different individuals can be compared (how do we compare the urges of the passionate person with the pallid preferences of the Stoic or suppressed personality?); whether animal interests or the interests of future people matter and how much; what should be maximised; how we should assess wants that an individual has suppressed or downgraded because of lack of opportunity to satisfy them or the preferences he has acquired because of oppression or distortions of personality. Utilitarians sometimes insist that we should take into account the preferences individuals actually have (Hare 1963: 118). But apart from problems about unconscious desires, this limitation is going to be controversial in those cases where we have reason to believe that satisfying preferences which an individual has downgraded will make him able to live a more satisfying life. Differences of opinion about this and other matters are likely to affect how utilitarians judge particular cases or generalise from their judgments, and it would be overly optimistic to suppose that they could all be settled if we had more information or were more rational. Even archangels could find themselves at loggerheads over the issues.

Another possible way of improving Rawls' method, making it more precise, and thus more likely to generate agreement, is to add further criteria for assessing observations and hypotheses. Norman Daniels (1979) claims that this early procedure of Rawls aims merely for a 'narrow reflective equilibrium'. It explicates ethical evidence by reference to generalisations and uses observations to test generalisations and vice versa. He argues that the method advocated in Rawls' *A Theory of Justice*, 'wide reflective equilibrium', provides a more sophisticated and satisfactory way of testing moral judgments. Moral principles are to be judged not only in relation to observations but by reference to well-supported background theories about morality, psychology and society. Wide reflective equilibrium aims to produce coherence between observations, principles and background theories, and the right principles are those supported by the most coherent system. Daniels thinks that this method is analogous to the way hypotheses are judged in science by reference to background theories (which are in turn supported by other theories and observations), and although he does not suppose that wide reflective equilibrium will resolve all ethical differences of opinion, he claims that 'it may increase our ability to choose among competing moral conceptions' (Daniels 1979: 257).

Why should we believe that forcing moral justification to jump through one more hoop will be an effective way of reducing dissonance? People who disagree about common moral issues are also likely to disagree on principles and either hold different background theories or use them differently. Those who hold the same background theories and principles can nevertheless disagree about their application or on what they think is relevant and important about the background theories. The reason why Daniels thinks that something can be accomplished by attention to background theories is probably because some of them are likely to be empirical theories about the nature of persons or society. If a moral view depends on an empirical theory, then knowing whether this theory is true or false could be a decisive reason for an ethical choice.

However, the bearing of empirical information on ethical theory is itself a matter of controversy. Bernard Williams (1981: 14ff.) argues, for example, that some moral theories are unviable because they do not allow individuals to pursue their own fundamental projects and thus undermine their ability to lead a meaningful life. Owen Flanagan, on the other hand, makes a distinction between moral requirements that would be overly demanding for individuals who have had their personalities and expectations shaped by a particular culture and moral demands which no human being could reasonably be expected to meet (Flanagan 1991: 32, 56). He thinks that Williams' argument is only applicable to people who have our cultural expectations and predispositions. A moralist could coherently, even reasonably, insist that we ought to do what we can to change ourselves and our culture. Flanagan supports what he calls the 'Principle of Minimal Psychological Realism', which requires only that a moral theory or ideal should be possible for creatures like us, and argues that this position rules out very little as far as moral theory is concerned (1991: 69ff.). If he is right, then empirical theory will not be of much help in reducing diversity of moral opinion. In any case, he shows that ethical theorists can also be at loggerheads about the implications of empirical information. This does not mean that empirical considerations are irrelevant or that it is a mistake to aim for a wide reflective equilibrium. What it suggests is that wide reflective equilibrium widens, rather than narrows, the range of issues on which ethical agents can disagree.

I have not proved that there is no way of reaching agreement about matters of controversy in ethics. I have reminded readers of what everyone knows: that disagreements in ethics are deep, extensive and infect every level of decision-making. I have also tried to show that neither ideal agency theories nor familiar ethical decision-procedures give us reason to think that they can be resolved, even in principle. Ethical rationality remains under siege.

However, it might be objected that it is premature to bemoan the failure of ethical epistemology to provide a solution to the problem of disagreement. There is an alternative idea of method that has not yet been considered. Jürgen Habermas argues that the procedures and approaches to ethical knowledge which I have examined in this chapter are all 'monolog-ical'. All of them suppose that what is right or wrong can and should be determined by the individual – whether that individual is an ideal agent or merely a competent judge. He thinks that monological approaches to ethics are all mistaken and advocates a dialogic approach which he calls discourse, or communicative, ethics. Habermas is not the only philosopher who advo-cates an interactive, discursive approach to making ethical judgments. His criticism of monology is joined by others who think that procedures which depend upon an ideal observer or even a competent judge are incapable of obtaining the insights necessary for good judgment. We need to determine what discourse ethics is, how it differs from methods so far examined, and whether it can better deal with the problem of dissonance.

2

DISCOURSE ETHICS AND THE CRITIQUE OF MONOLOGY

Habermas' views about ethics arise out of a criticism of Kantian transcendentalism and a rejection of correspondence theories of truth. Discourse ethics, according to Seyla Benhabib, is Kantian ethics collectivised.

> Instead of asking what an individual moral agent could or would will, without contradiction, to be a universal maxim for all, one asks: what norms or institutions would the members of an ideal or real communication community agree to as representing their common interests after engaging in a special kind of argumentation or conversation? The procedural model of an argumentative praxis replaces the silent thought-experiment enjoined by Kantian universalisability.
>
> (Benhabib 1990: 331)

Agreement in discourse has to replace conclusions reached by individual reflection because there is no such thing as the transcendental rational will with a licence to legislate for the whole of human kind. Humanity as a whole is the only subject with the authority to determine the moral law for humanity.

Agreement is also required because the truth of moral, as well as non-moral, propositions depends upon it. Habermas rejects the idea that propositions are made true by their relation to reality (inner or outer), and adopts instead a consensus theory of truth. What is right is determined by what can universally be agreed to in discourse. Kant's universalisability requirement, the categorical imperative, must thus be replaced by a meta-ethical principle which makes acceptance requirements clear. Every valid norm, says Habermas, has to fulfil the requirement U: that 'all affected can accept the consequences and the side effects its general observance can be anticipated to have for the satisfaction of everyone's interests (and these consequences are preferred to those of known alternative possibilities for regulation)' (Habermas 1990: 65).

This conception of ethical truth (or as Habermas prefers to say, 'rightness') is not undermined by a failure of individuals to reach agreement; nor is it satisfied by any agreement individuals happen to reach. In his earlier works Habermas defined truth as the consensus individuals would reach in an ideal speech situation, where all limitations on reasoning and knowledge, physical, psychological and social are removed (Habermas 1979: 119–20). In the ideal speech situation participation is not limited by time and space, and participants are therefore able to bring to bear on any view presented to them all the considerations and knowledge that creatures like us are capable of acquiring. The conclusions they reach are not affected by prejudice, oppressive social relations or the distorting influences that some people exercise over others. In the ideal speech situation people are equal in competence and are freed from all intellectual disabilities and psychological or social repression. So constituted, they will accept only those conclusions which are supported by the strength of the best reasons.

Discourse and agreement

Habermas' appeal to an ideal speech situation is a version of ideal agency theory, and it encounters the same predicament. If the individuals who are supposed to reach agreement by discourse are so different from us, it is difficult to know whether their reasoning has any bearing on our ethical or epistemological concerns, or whether they would have ethical concerns or be able to make ethical decisions. Would a person without any kind of psychological repression have a personality at all? Would individuals who are equal in knowledge, status, competence, etc. have anything to discuss? In Habermas' later works ideal discourse is conceived as a limit rather than as an imaginable situation or utopian goal (1992: 145). Real people in real discourses can approach this ideal by becoming more rational, by including more points of view, eliminating prejudice, gaining knowledge, etc. But in ethics as in science we will never reach a point where we are justified in believing that all errors, biases and other distortions have been eliminated. Real individuals can only aspire to rationally justified belief.

However, this understanding of the ideal speech situation gives rise to the other difficulty which plagues ideal agency theories. Why should we suppose that individuals, even when they are doing what they can to approach the ideal, will reach a consensus about right? Why should we suppose that universal consensus is possible under the best conditions that human reasoners can achieve? Why should we even suppose that discourse *tends* towards consensus? Habermas has to be able to answer these questions if he is to show that discourse ethics is able to do what monological approaches cannot do: ground the claim that ethical consensus is possible in principle. Given his endorsement of a consensus theory of truth, the problem of disagreement is a central difficulty for his theory and we must have reason to think that he can solve it.

Consensus in ethics is possible, Habermas argues, because ethics, like science, is a wholly rational enterprise. Emotivists, relativists, nihilists and other sceptics about ethical judgment are wrong. The role that ethics plays in our lives: the seriousness with which we respond to the actions we judge wrong, our insistence that moral judgments be justified, the presumption that morality is something we ought to reason about – all of these familiar features of ethical life and discourse indicate that we do not, and cannot, regard our ethical utterances as mere expressions of feeling or attempts to manipulate others. Ethical judgments, he concludes, must be treated as knowledge claims and ethical disputes are (or can be) serious attempts to determine what is right (Habermas 1990: 45ff.).[1] This means, he thinks, that in ethics as in science, progress towards agreement can be achieved as inquiry becomes more rational, better informed and less affected by distorting influences. Discourse makes this progress possible by ensuring that anyone who has anything to contribute to an inquiry is able to participate in it.

There are two problems with Habermas' defence of ethical rationality. The first is that he, like many other ethical theorists, does not do justice to the considerations which give rise to scepticism about ethical judgment. To point out that we take our ethical judgments seriously and reason about them is not enough to show that non-rationalism or relativism is wrong. For we also have to take into account the outside view of our judgments: the perspective that forces us to acknowledge that agreement among agents is often not forthcoming, however rational they try to be. The second difficulty is that even if a closer examination of ethical judgments vindicates the inside view, this does not mean that we can expect from ethical inquiry the same progress towards agreement that is possible in science. Habermas is assuming that inquiry in ethics requires the same rationality and can expect the same outcome as scientific inquiry. How can he make this assumption? Why should we suppose that he has a better answer to the problem of disagreement than other ethical theorists who go down the same path?

These questions are supposed to be answered by his theory of communicative action. 'Reaching understanding is the inherent *telos* of human speech', says Habermas (1984: 287) (at least of that speech which is not manipulative or the expression of feelings). When we make a judgment we are performing a communicative action, whether we are actually conversing with another or merely thinking something out for ourselves. Every act of communication presupposes that certain conditions are satisfied (whether we are aware of these conditions or not). If I ask someone for a glass of water, I am tacitly making claims, empirical, normative and expressive (1984: 305–8). My utterance presupposes that there is water to be had, that I am entitled to request it, and that I am sincere in my request. If others question one or more of these claims, then fulfilling the *telos* of communication requires that I satisfy them in a way that enables an understanding to be achieved. This means that I must try to persuade them through good reasons and rational arguments that I am justified in claiming what I do. More generally, we achieve understanding and thus satisfy the requirements of communicative action if and only if we, as rational agents, come to an agreement about what is right or true. 'Processes of reaching understanding aim at an agreement that meets the conditions of rationally motivated assent' (1984: 287).

The requirements of rationality, whether for ethics or science, do not, according to Habermas' theory, depend upon what we happen to think is rational. They are not merely the prescriptions of a decision-procedure. Like rules of grammar they exist whether we know them or not, whether we follow them or not. Since ethical judgments are supposed to be communicative acts (and since some of the tacit claims made by other kinds of utterance are also normative), they are subject to the same requirements. If they are questioned, they must be justified to the satisfaction of all participants in inquiry, and the *telos* of communication will not be achieved until consensus is reached.

Let us suppose that Habermas' theory of communicative action is right: that our speech acts make validity claims which, if questioned, have to be justified in a discourse that aims at agreement. However, this theory does not establish that ethical utterances can be rationally justified; nor does it establish that consensus concerning ethical issues is possible. It assumes rather than proves that ethical judgment can be rational. His appeal to ethical phenomenology – the fact that we take seriously demands for ethical justification – presupposes what needs to proved: that the inside view of our moral judgments is correct. A sceptic might argue that ethical propositions are really more like expressive utterances, or that they are really acts of manipulation – that is, not the sort of thing that we are required to justify in discourse. Or it might be argued that ethical standards are conventional norms like the rules of etiquette and that reaching ethical agreement is a very different exercise, or has a very different purpose, from reaching agreement about scientific judgments. The theory of communicative action does not exclude these possibilities. Furthermore it does not guarantee that the *telos* of communication can be realised in the case of ethics. Individuals with all the rational will in the world may not end up with just one rational will. The dissonance between inside and outside views of ethical judgment may be the result of expectations which in the case of ethics cannot be fulfilled. Habermas' theory of communicative action does not provide a reason for thinking that discourse ethics is better equipped to solve the problem of disagreement than other approaches to ethical judgment.

Why discourse?

Habermas is a critic of what he calls 'monology': the idea that an individual by himself or herself can determine the truth or falsity of an ethical proposition. He objects not merely to the extreme versions of monology embodied in ideal observer theories, but to decision-procedures which hand over to competent judges the responsibility for ethical inquiry. Even Rawls' contractual approach to the theory of justice is rejected by Habermas. For Rawls thinks that individuals in the original position will go through the same reasoning and come to the same conclusion, and therefore that one individual could satisfactorily represent the views of everyone (1973: 139). Habermas, on the contrary, believes that ethical inquiry is essential 'dialogic'. Discourse is supposed to be central to his ethical method in a way that it is not central to the methods of Hare, Rawls, Daniels and others discussed in Chapter 1. Habermas claims to be advocating a different approach to ethical theory and decision-making, and any investigation of the nature of ethical reasoning has to determine what the difference is and what it means for ethical inquiry. So let us assume that the objective of reaching agreement is not an impossible goal, and concentrate our attention on the question of why discourse is supposed to be necessary for achieving it.

In Habermas' view, there is nothing epistemologically special about ethics. It is no more inherently dialogic than is science. All inquiry requires discourse which aims at consensus, and what counts as empirical truths are also the conclusions which knowledgeable, rational inquirers would reach in an ideal speech situation. Habermas sometimes presents himself as defending a fallibalistic idea of inquiry: one which requires that we regard ourselves, both in our ethical and empirical investigations, as being participants in an ongoing community of inquiry dedicated to the critical scrutiny of the hypotheses and observations made by each other and by our predecessors. Nothing is supposed to be regarded as beyond question. However, this idea of inquiry is widely held (including by those, like Karl Popper and W.V.O. Quine, who do not endorse a consensus theory of truth), and it is compatible with the methods of ethical inquiry advocated by Rawls, Daniels and most other contemporary moral philosophers. Indeed, Rawls, and especially Daniels, are attempting to adapt for ethics an idea of inquiry which stresses the revisability of all ethical judgments as well as the background assumptions which inform them.

If Habermas is simply endorsing a view of rationality which is already accepted by many empirical and ethical theorists and embedded in their ideas of method, then how can he think that discourse ethics is different from, and superior to, the 'monological' procedures he criticises? The answer must be found in the features of Habermas' position which distinguish it from other approaches: the consensus theory of truth, the theory of communicative action, or his adoption of the meta-ethical principle 'U'. I will argue that none of these require discourse to have a role which is different from the role it plays in other ethical procedures.

The consensus theory of truth, considered in itself, is not capable of explaining why Habermas thinks that ethics, or for that matter, empirical science, is essentially dialogic. The consensus theory says that a proposition is true if and only if it would be agreed to in an ideal speech situation. It doesn't say how that agreement is reached. It is compatible with the theory that the agreement be reached by each individual reasoning to a conclusion on their own (as imagined by Rawls in *A Theory of Justice*). It is compatible with the idea that there could be an ideal observer who determines by herself what conclusion individuals would agree to in the ideal speech situation. And the definition of truth as consensus under certain circumstances is compatible with the method of wide reflective equilibrium. Participants in inquiry can regard themselves as using this method to approach the consensus which would be reached in the ideal speech situation.

Habermas' theory of communicative action requires that those who make statements with the object of communication be prepared to clarify and justify the explicit or implicit claims made by their utterances if these are brought into question. Justification, he insists, is essentially a dialogic activity. However, 'justification' can mean different things. It can stand for the process of determining what we ought to believe, or it can mean what we are supposed to do if our views are questioned. The second is clearly a dialogic activity (though there is no reason why the dialogue can't be with oneself). It does not follow that dialogue is necessary for the first kind of justification: that discourse is necessary to ethical inquiry itself. It does not follow that monological methods, even ideal observer theories, are mistaken. An ideal observer, if questioned, would have to justify her conclusions to others. If the observer could not do this, then we would doubt whether her 'knowledge' or way of knowing was relevant to our epistemological concerns. However, this does not mean that the observer's knowledge or ability to know that she knows is dependent on discourse.

For creatures like us, confidence in our beliefs sometimes depends upon confirmation that can only occur through dialogue with others. We rely on information and ideas that others may be in a better position to supply. We depend on their ability to criticise our beliefs and correct our errors. These are familiar reasons for wanting to engage in dialogue or having that possibility open. However, this idea of the place of dialogue does not seem any different from the role it is given in most accounts of scientific method or in common views about ethical decision-making. The decision-procedures for competent judges described by Rawls, Daniels and others either explicitly or implicitly incorporate critical discourse. Rawls supposes that competent judges discuss and criticise each others' performances and 'hypotheses', and thus help each other to arrive at conclusions which all can accept.[2] Daniels insists that all ethical observations, theories and background assumptions are open to question and criticism. Their methods are equally 'dialogic'.

It might be argued that Habermas' requirement 'U': that an ethical generalisation cannot be regarded as right unless those affected are willing to accept the generalisation, does make dialogue essential. For how else but through dialogue can we determine whether people accept a particular principle or judgment? However, what is morally important (as Habermas would agree) is not what people happen to accept, but what they *should* accept. There seems to be no reason why a well-positioned ethical judge, Hare's archangel, perhaps, could not know what rational individuals would agree on (if anything). Habermas' principle seems very similar to Scanlon's insistence that we should aim for principles about which no one can reasonably disagree. But Scanlon does not make any prescription about how we are to achieve this. There seems to be no reason why a method like that of Rawls or Daniels, or Rawls' procedure in *A Theory of Justice*, could not be adopted as a way of determining the principles which reasonable people would not reject.

So far we have found nothing in Habermas' position which justifies his claim that his approach to ethics is essentially different from the approaches he labels 'monological'. Discourse plays the same role in the procedures of Daniels and Rawls and others as it does in his discourse ethics. Nevertheless, there is clearly a difference in emphasis between Habermas' approach and the positions he criticises. Rawls and Daniels incorporate discourse into their methods and mention it now and then, but they don't have much to say about it. For Habermas it takes the centre of the stage. This difference in presentation is, I believe, the result of different interests.

Most views about ethical decision-making are 'synchronic': they are supposed to enable individuals, situated as they are in time and place, with the knowledge and sensibility that they now have, to reach reasonable conclusions about right. Synchronicity is most in evidence in Rawls' *Theory of Justice* where he assumes that individuals behind the veil of ignorance have background knowledge about psychology and social affairs available to reasonably well-informed people of their time (1973: 137–8). The relevance and validity of this information is simply taken for granted. Neither Rawls, nor anyone else, would want to claim that these background assumptions cannot be criticised and rejected, or that the ethical views arrived at by his method would not be affected by changes to our background knowledge.[3] However, since Rawls is concerned with the agreements people in a particular type of society can now reach about principles of justice, he is prepared to make the assumption that this background information is as correct and complete as it needs to be.

Habermas' discourse ethics is 'diachronic': it emphasises how background assumptions, theories and moral principles are revised and developed in response to criticisms, changes in sensibility and new ideas. It emphasises ethical change and the evolutionary development of ethical understanding. This undoubtedly explains why discourse plays a more up-front role in his view of ethical reasoning. For ethical change is generally brought about through communication and criticism. However, we have no reason to suppose that this difference of emphasis amounts to an alternative ethical decision-making method, and thus no reason for thinking that Habermas' approach to ethics is any less monological than other approaches (or that they are any more monological).

Some purposes of discourse

In his recent criticisms of Rawls and other moral theorists Habermas presents further arguments for the claim that discourse has a role in ethical decision-making which is different from its role in 'monological' decision-procedures. Other advocates of discourse, including some feminists and political philosophers, have also presented reasons for thinking that dialogue ought to feature more prominently in moral and political decision-making – though they do not always have the same ideas as Habermas about the nature and purpose of ethical or political inquiry. I will examine these demands for discourse and their implications for accounts of ethical ratio-nality.

Habermas' first argument begins with the observation that no one can comprehend everyone else's perspective and interests or be sure that she has judged them impartially. Kant's universalisation test, he says, cannot be carried out in a monological fashion in a pluralistic world (Habermas 1995: 117). This means that discourse is necessary to 'enlarge' each individual's interpretive perspective, as well as to criticise biases and prejudices.

However, this function of discourse, as we have seen, is also recognised by the approaches to ethics which Habermas regards as 'monological'. In his early decision-procedure Rawls supposes that competent judges will conduct a dialogue with those whose case is being judged, and though he does not say anything about the right of appeal for those not satisfied that a judge has understood their interests or judged them impartially, this is some-thing that could easily be incorporated into the procedure. Brandt's cognitive psychotherapy involves being open to criticisms of others and learning how to appreciate fully their interests and points of view, something that would be difficult to accomplish without dialogue. A utilitarian judge less perfect than Hare's archangel will often find it necessary to consult others about their interests and will have to take into account criticisms of the way that she does this.

Nevertheless, it could be argued that there is an important difference between an epistemological model which features a disinterested, imper-sonal ideal agent or an authoritative, detached ethical judge, and one which regards as central discourse among people who are concerned to solve their own ethical problems. Margaret Urban Walker claims that the standard images and analogies used in ethical epistemology have a detrimental effect on our understanding of what moral reasoning requires. The ideal observer is essentially a spectator, and the competent judge, made as she is in the image of the judicial judge, interacts with those whose cases she judges only in a limited, regimented way. Philosophers who use these images of the ethical agent are inclined to think that the difficult task of understanding the interests and concerns of others is a purely imaginative exercise – a matter of 'thinking *for* others'. What we have to do instead is 'think *with* others'. 'Asking, telling, repeating, mutually clarifying, mulling over, and checking back are the most dependable, accessible, and efficient devices for finding out how it is with others . . . ' (Walker 1991: 768–9).[4] This suggests that discourse ethics, because of its emphasis on engagement with others, provides a more appropriate idea of ethical inquiry.

Some feminist critics make similar complaints about ethical decision-procedures which rely on the judgments of 'impartial' observers. Seyla Benhabib thinks that these procedures, and the ethical generalisations which come out of them, treat individuals abstractly: the detached observer comprehends individuals according to the categories which she brings to judgment. The interests, feelings, points of view of *concrete* individuals can only be adequately represented and understood in a discourse in which they speak for themselves. 'Without engagement, confrontation, dialogue and even a "struggle for recognition" in the Hegelian sense, we tend to constitute the otherness of the other by projection and fantasy, or ignore it in indifference' (Benhabib 1992: 168). Lynne S. Arnault thinks that Hare's requirement for good moral judgment – that we become well-acquainted enough with others so that we can understand how things are from their point of view – can only be achieved by 'actual dialogic interaction with concrete others' (Arnault 1989: 197). No detached individual, even an archangel, can be trusted or expected to comprehend the position of everyone.

An ethical inquiry which emphasises discourse, according to these criticisms, is superior because discourse enables ethical reasoners to understand the feelings, attitudes and points of view of others by direct, intimate conversational engagement. Furthermore, it allows individuals to enter into a discussion about how the case that they are involved in should be judged. An ethics which emphasises discourse does not give the expert or the detached observer a licence to pass judgments which others are bound to accept as authoritative. Walker and other critics are, perhaps, too dismissive of the ethical judge conceived as an independent observer. Sometimes those who are not directly engaged in solving a problem, or who are observers rather than participants in ethical conversation, can recognise motives and perceive needs that might not be evident even to those who have the motives or the needs. They may detect biases which are not noticed by those directly concerned. There is a place for detachment and observation. However, let us assume that Walker and other advocates of discourse are right: the best way, perhaps the only way, for us to determine what others need and want, or how they understand a situation and what they think is right is to engage in an ongoing conversation with them (and not just to consult them from time to time).

However, this function of discourse is not fundamentally incompatible with decision-procedures like those of Rawls or Daniels. If it were to be incorporated into these procedures some of the requirements would have to be changed. The criticisms of Walker and others suggest that the relation between an ethical inquirer and the objects of his or her inquiry (which could include his or her own actions) is different from the relation between observer and observed in most cases of scientific inquiry. Detached observation has to be replaced by conversational engagement; the ethical inquirers will include those whose case is being judged, and methods of inquiry will have to provide means by which ethical actors can become aware of, and learn to appreciate, the views of those who have conflicting interests (which will undoubtedly involve discourse, but also, possibly, other techniques). These changes do not mean that the nature, purpose or rationality of the procedure has been altered. The inquirers will still be making judgments about particular cases on the basis of their observations (which can include the information they get from discourse), they will be making generalisations and testing them through further observations and the criticisms of others. There is no reason to think that a procedure which incorporates discourse in the way described differs in an epistemologically important respect from 'monological' approaches.

The second reason why Habermas thinks that discourse is necessary for determining the validity of norms is that moral principles are an expression of the common will.

> If moral argument is to produce this kind of agreement it is not enough for the individual to reflect on whether he can assent to a norm. It is not even enough for each individual to reflect in this way and then to register his vote. What is needed is a real process of argumentation in which the individuals concerned co-operate. Only an intersubjective process of reaching understanding can produce an agreement that is reflexive in nature; only it can give the participants the knowledge that they have collectively become convinced of something.
>
> (Habermas 1990: 67)[5]

Moral principles cannot be the basis for co-operation, he seems to be saying, unless each of us publicly assents to them and knows that the others do so too (and knows that they do so for the right reasons).[6]

This reason for thinking that discourse is essential can once again be traced back to Habermas' theory of communicative action. Agreement is the '*telos* of communication', according to that theory because reaching an understanding is fundamental to our ability to maintain a 'life world': the assumptions, interpretations, values and responses which we share and which make co-operation possible. Since such understandings can only exist if they are both shared and known to be shared, misunderstanding, dissent and disagreement have to be addressed and resolved to the satisfaction of those concerned.

Habermas' concern with requirements that must be fulfilled if co-operation is to be possible makes his position similar in some respects to the view John Rawls defends in *Political Liberalism* (1996: Part One). Rawls' concern is how groups of people with different rational comprehensive doctrines (such as different religious beliefs) can arrive at an overlapping consensus about the basic principles of their society. The consensus Rawls thinks they should aspire to is not a mere *modus vivendi*: a political compromise. Each group is supposed to accept the overlapping consensus as a fair basis for co-operation for reasons that can be found in its particular comprehensive doctrine. Habermas' theory focuses on how an already existing basis for co-operation is maintained or modified in the face of dissent and misunderstanding. Rawls provides an account of how a common position can be achieved by people who have different moral views of the world. However, both seem to be offering pragmatic theories about the achievement of co-operation based upon consent, and discourse is clearly central to both accounts. For Rawls, finding and endorsing an overlapping consensus would require discussion among members of each group and among their representatives. Indeed, he says that public discussion among reasonable citizens who 'take one another into account as having reasonable comprehensive doctrines that endorse [the political conception of justice]' is an essential part of the procedure of justifying a view of justice (Rawls 1995: 143).[7]

However, Rawls insists that political liberalism is about finding a political consensus, and not about determining what is true from a moral point of view. People with different rational comprehensive doctrines do not have to bring into question the tenents of their faith or the premises of their moral doctrines in order to achieve an overlapping consensus; they do not even have to suppose that the principles agreed to constitute moral truths. Whether they do regard them as true will depend not on the procedure for achieving consensus but on whether they can find a basis for them in their own comprehensive views. Rawls makes a firm distinction between the criteria for making a good political agreement and the criteria an individual might use for judging that a moral belief is true.

The crucial question is why Habermas and Rawls, who seem to have very similar pragmatic objectives, make such different claims about the epistemological (and ontological) significance of agreement through discourse. One important difference between the two is that Habermas is not merely interested in agreement on political principles. The life world which we depend on, and have to co-operate to maintain, encompasses our everyday interactions and all aspects of our lives. Every communication has to be understood in relation to it, and therefore any dissent or failure to understand requires discursive attention. Nevertheless, the distinction that Rawls makes between reasonable or principled consensus and what an individual believes is right (and the method he uses to do determine this) seems to apply to these wider spheres of co-operation, especially when moral matters are involved. People who recognise that they disagree on many moral issues from abortion to the nature of justice and do not think that they will easily be able to resolve their disagreements (or who think that agreement cannot be achieved) may maintain co-operation (depending on the context) by agreeing to tolerate each other's point of view, or by avoiding all discussion of controversial issues, by stressing what they are able to agree on, or by constructing an overlapping consensus. All of these could be regarded as principled ways of dealing with difference, ways that may be satisfactory to all concerned. However, no one would confuse these pragmatic means of achieving co-operation in the face of difference with an agreement about what is morally right. If the *telos* of communication is indeed agreement for the sake of co-operation, then Habermas' theory of communicative action seems best interpreted as a pragmatic theory about how to achieve fair co-operation – and not as a theory about how to determine what is right. The fact that Habermas gives us no good reason to believe that people will be able to reach an agreement through discourse about what is morally right provides a further motivation for this interpretation of his theory.

The third reason why Habermas thinks that discourse is necessary is that the needs and interests of individuals, which 'U' – Habermas' universalisability principle – requires moral agents to take into account, cannot be regarded as fixed and given. Since these interests are interpreted in the light of cultural values and 'cultural values are always components of intersubjectively shared traditions, the revision of values used to interpret needs and wants cannot be a matter for individuals to handle monologically' (Habermas 1990: 67–8). Habermas seems to be complaining that procedures like those of Rawls or Daniels require that judges take interests as given, and are not able to encompass changes in desires. What is required, it seems, is a discourse in which both interests of individuals and questions of right and wrong are discussed at the same time.

However, Habermas' reasoning does not establish this. Let us grant that interests of individuals are subject to change and re-interpretation as their culture and social life changes, and that culture is (to some extent) the product of their collective wills (though Habermas seems to overstate the extent to which cultural changes are deliberately and collectively brought about). But this consideration doesn't undermine the decision-procedures of Rawls or Daniels or show that their conclusions are mistaken. If moral judgment depends on what interests individuals have, and these interests change or are re-interpreted, then we may have to judge future cases differently from the way we judged similar cases in the past, and our principles may also have to be altered. However, this is not a reason for abandoning Rawls' procedure. Once again, it seems appropriate to view the difference between Habermas and those whom he accuses of being monological as a difference between a diachronic and synchronic view of ethics and not a difference in ethical method.

Habermas can, however be interpreted as making the more radical suggestion that considerations of right and determinations of interests cannot be separated: moral reasoning is not only affected by our interests, but our interests change in the course of moral reasoning.[8] Let us assume that by 'interests' he means the non-moral objectives and values of individuals and groups. (Moral interests are, after all, the kind of thing that moral reasoning *is* supposed to determine or alter.) The kind of investigation which moral reasoning requires could encourage individuals to change their interests. By learning more about what others think and do I may change my mind about how I should live my life or what objectives I should aim for. Others' 'experiments in living' may influence my choices. Nevertheless, these changes of interest, like the changes that result from cultural re-interpretation, can be taken into account by so called 'monological' methods.

A more radical interpretation of Habermas' idea of ethical reasoning seems incoherent. If what is right is determined by what individual interests are, then it seems that interests have to be fixed, at least for the time being, if any moral conclusion is going to be reached. This does not mean that they have to be fixed all at once or forever, or that moral judges step in when individuals have stopped reflecting on or discussing their objectives. All of us are moral judges and all of us have interests and values, and we reflect upon both as we live our lives. Models like those of Rawls and Daniels simply isolate, and focus our attention on, moral reasoning itself. Habermas gives us no reason for thinking that this cannot or should not be done.

The arguments of Habermas and others for the claim that discourse should be more central to ethical decision-making than allowed for by procedures he criticises as 'monological' are not successful. Habermas' discourse ethics, and other appeals to discourse, do not provide a substantive alternative to these procedures. Discourse ethics is compatible with, if not exactly the same as, the procedures advocated by Rawls and Daniels, and it encounters the same difficulties. The reason why it is not essentially different is because it makes the same basic assumption about how ethical knowledge is obtained. Habermas and other advocates of discourse share with Rawls, Daniels and advocates of ideal observer theories the belief that an individual possesses, or can come to possess, the epistemological resources necessary for making a moral judgment which she is justified in believing is right. Discourse is supposed to put an individual into the position where she can make such judgments. It corrects her mistakes, points out her prejudices, supplies her with information and hypotheses that can only come from contact with others. But in the end it is up to the individual to determine for herself what is true or false, right or wrong. Reaching consensus would simply mean that each individual is able to arrive at the same judgment. The agreement they aim at is assumed to be a distributive one. So it is no surprise that Habermas' discourse ethics is no less monological than the approaches he criticises, and they are (at least potentially) no less dialogic. The failure of defenders of discourse ethics to provide a real alternative to standard accounts of ethical rationality raises the question of whether there is another way of giving a content to the distinction between a monological and a dialogic approach to ethical reasoning. In the next chapters I will argue that an alternative does exist, and I will present and defend a truly dialogic ethics.

The motivation for doing this is the unsolved problem of disagreement. Habermas, no less than other moral philosophers, faces the problem of reconciling inside and outside perspectives on ethical judgment, of explaining why we should aim for consensus when there is no reason for thinking that it is possible to reach it. Since he thinks that the existence of ethical truth *depends* upon reaching agreement, he is particularly vulnerable to the doubts of subjectivists and nihilists. To understand the problem of disagreement and make any progress towards resolving it, we need to have a better understanding of why rational agents so often fail to agree about ethical matters. In Chapter 3 I will try to answer this question and show that a proper appreciation of the nature and limitations of ethical judgment supports the method for reaching conclusions and resolving disputes which I call ethical collectivism.

3

THE NATURE OF MORAL JUDGMENT: A MORAL-PSYCHOLOGICAL INQUIRY

Moral disagreement is not merely a familiar fact of life. For all their efforts, moral philosophers have not succeeded in showing how persistent disagreement can be overcome by monological means – even in principle. The obvious question is why moral dissonance is so prevalent: why it is that disagreement about moral matters, unlike the debates of scientists about the empirical world, are so seldom resolved. However, there is another equally important question which must also be answered. Why is it that we think that moral dissonance should be resolved or transcended? Why are we not content to believe that there is no truth of the matter as far as ethical beliefs are concerned? Why instead do we insist on trying to comprehend and argue against the positions of those who have different views? An adequate account of the nature of moral judgment must explain, or explain away, both our disagreements and our belief that we ought to be able to agree.

What is the problem?

The answer to the question, 'why do we disagree?', must lie either in our own shortcomings or in the nature of moral judgment itself. Given the failure of decision-procedures and ideal agency theory to show that consensus among rational agents is possible, it seems reasonable to conclude that not all moral disagreements can all be attributed to prejudices, bad reasoning, lack of information, etc. Nevertheless, I have not *proved* that this is so. John Pollock and others who claim that we disagree in our moral opinions because moral judgment is especially difficult could turn out to be right. Indeed, this idea about the source of the problem is given support by the considerations advanced by Walker, Arnault, Benhabib and others who stress the importance of understanding the points of view of those involved in a moral situation. This understanding is clearly difficult to achieve. Even if we can engage others in discourse, there are going to be barriers to communication. An individual's ability to comprehend the thoughts and feelings of others is affected by his own situation: his upbringing, social environment, outlook and personal propensities. Iris Marion Young sometimes

46

makes the stronger claim that difference of situation does not merely make 'true and complete' understanding difficult. It makes it impossible. ' . . . One subject cannot fully empathise with another in a different social location, adopt her point of view' (Young 1990: 105). If she is right then it looks like we don't have to look any further to explain why moral agents persistently disagree in their judgments.

However, the problem of comprehension, though it clearly exists, does not seem insurmountable. In fact, Young, as an advocate of discourse, thinks that individuals can find ways of communicating their experiences and views, and that others are able to understand them – providing these others properly and patiently attend to what is being communicated. People can learn to appreciate the feelings and views of others sufficiently well, at least, to satisfy these others that they have been understood. The objective is, after all, not to experience the feelings and thoughts of another person – which is truly impossible – but to understand how he or she sees his interests and what he regards as important: something that he should be able to communicate or reveal in one way or another. Indeed, his attempts to communicate with others and be understood by them, may (sometimes) be the best means he can employ to understand himself and his situation.[1]

In any case, the making of moral judgments does not always require that we know others intimately. People can have well-supported opinions about the justice of a particular social policy without discussions with everyone affected by the policy. I can judge that the massacre of Aborigines by British settlers in Australia was wrong without close acquaintance with the thoughts, attitudes and objectives of the people involved (although historical knowledge about actions and motivations may deepen my understanding of the nature of the wrong and why these wrong actions occurred). Acquaintance with the thoughts and feelings of concrete individuals who are involved in situations being judged is not always necessary to good moral judgments, and if it were made a requirement it would get in the way of our making judgments which we think we are entitled to make.[2]

These considerations make it less plausible to suppose that all moral disagreement (that cannot be attributed to irrationality of moral judges) results from failures of understanding. However, the most serious problem with the suggestion that we disagree in our moral judgments because understanding others is difficult is that this hypothesis does not seem to explain our most persistent disputes. Individuals can participate in the same discourses, become acquainted equally well with a moral problem and the people involved, be equally familiar with the thoughts and feelings of these people – and yet make different moral judgments. The person who judges that abortion is wrong may be just as well-acquainted as his opponents with the points of view of women who have unwanted pregnancies. Those who oppose his position might claim that he lacks a *real* understanding of the feelings of these women, but if there is no evidence for supposing that he lacks compassion or information or that he has failed to communicate, then this accusation seems to be nothing more than a way of saying that they think he is wrong.

A failure to understand another person's situation or point of view is different from a failure to agree with his or her moral opinions. A husband may understand why his wife wants and needs a relationship with another man, and the wife may understand her husband's feelings of jealousy and abandonment. The couple may have an intimate and sympathetic knowledge of each other's feelings and attitudes, and yet disagree about whether adultery, in this case or any other, is wrong. Though there is no way of proving beyond the possibility of doubt that those who think that moral disagreement can be attributed to a lack of understanding, or other deficiencies of reason or person, are wrong, the prevalence of cases where intimacy or acquaintance with the points of view of others is not conducive to moral agreement suggests the need for some other explanation.

Subjectivists and sceptics think that they know what this explanation is. They claim that what I call the 'inside perspective on ethical judgment', the view that encourages us to think that our judgments are objective and rational, is simply wrong. Moral judgments, they say, are at bottom non-rational; they are reactions caused or influenced by the idiosyncratic nature of the individual – his emotions, commitments or ideology. Non-rationalists think that the foundations of ethical belief are epistemologically arbitrary. There is no way of justifying them, and thus, in the last analysis, there are no considerations which show that one ethical point of view is better than others. Non-rationalists have no difficulty explaining why people disagree, or, rather, appear to do so. Individuals often *do* differ in their commitments, emotional responses or ideologies, and this makes them judge differently. No amount of argument is going to persuade them to reach a consensus, but this is simply because no rationally achieved consensus is possible. We are wrong to think that we ought to be able to agree about moral matters.

I will argue that the subjectivists and sceptics are wrong about moral judgment. This will require a close examination of how ethical judgments are formed and justified, an account which enables us to understand how individuals can be rational and well-informed and yet end up with different conclusions about what ought to be done. My arguments will aim to show that we are right to think that our ethical judgments are, or can be, rational 'all the way down'. To this extent the inside view of ethical judgment is vindicated. However, the arguments which show that our judgments are rational do not demonstrate that they are also objective: that we are entitled to believe that they are right and that other rational agents should therefore accept them. A moral-psychological inquiry into the nature of ethical judgments reveals that they depend on a perspective which is the product of an individual's life history, his critical reflections on his experiences and how the experiences of others relate to them. Non-rationalism can be defeated, but at a price. For if judgment is non-objective then our ethical judgments cannot have the authority that moral agents and moral philosophers suppose them to have. A radical relativist accepts this result and insists that individuals, however rational, can only legislate for themselves about moral matters. I will argue, finally, that radical relativism cannot account for the reasons we have for wanting to take into account the views of others, and that it is, furthermore, an unstable and unsatisfactory position for other reasons. An investigation into the nature of our moral judgments, I will try to show, leads to the conclusion that ethical collectivism provides the most reasonable way of accommodating what is true about ethical judgment.

The challenge of non-rationalism

There are different ways of being a 'non-rationalist' about ethical judgment. Gilbert Harman (1984: 35) is inclined to think that the moral beliefs of individuals depend upon the 'social customs, practices, conventions, values, and principles that they accept'. Because of their upbringing and psychology individuals hold different basic moral assumptions, and once a debate about moral matters comes down to these basic premises reason won't take us any further.

Other non-rationalists place a greater emphasis on the idiosyncrasies of individual psychology. Moral response, they say, depends on the emotions or attitudes of the individual. 'Emotivism', as it is usually called, can take more or less sophisticated forms. Positivists were notorious for analysing moral judgments as a description of a matter of fact supplemented by a negative or positive attitude: 'A has pushed a knife into B. Bad!' But emotivists can allow that evaluation is epistemologically basic, that people who make moral judgments do not first determine the empirical facts and then react to them. They can allow that ethical judgments are not *merely* emotional reactions. They can admit that they are arguable propositions and that people can reason about ethical matters – up to a point. What all those describable as emotivists insist upon is that ethical judgment depends, at least partially, on what we feel about a situation, and that these feelings or attitudes are, in the last analysis, non-rational. So in examining an ethical opinion a critic will sooner or later come down to the emotional response on which the view depends, and he cannot reasonably claim that this reaction is an error. We feel what we feel. And since it seems likely that the emotional responses of individuals will sometimes be different, their resulting 'disagreements' are insurmountable – barring a change of personality, which itself is a non-rational development. For if emotivism is true, then consensus, even if brought about, cannot be an achievement of reason.

Other non-rationalists hold that ethical judgment is a commitment – a choice made beyond the reach of reasons. This view of ethical decision-making is often attributed to Sartre. When an individual faces a moral choice, he says, he is engaged in an act of creation – he is determining himself as a moral individual, and neither religion, moral systems, nor the advice of others can or should determine how he does this (1975: 354ff.). Not even his own emotional predispositions can dictate how he makes a particular decision. For he may decide to change himself and his moral life. Sartre is generally understood to be treating moral choice rather like commitment to a personal good or a course for one's life – like the decision to convert to a religion or to devote oneself to a political cause. An individual who makes such a choice will have his reasons, but has to acknowledge that they are not rationally compelling. Others in his position may not be moved at all by these reasons, and he himself knows that they do not *require* him to make the decision he makes. He could choose differently and still be as rational. Nor is his choice explained by his feelings or his upbringing. He may deliberately be acting out of character and against the grain of his inclinations. Moral decision-making, understood in this way, is at the frontier of the formation of the self. Since moral judgments as commitments are underdetermined by reasons, it is not surprising (according to this view) that people faced with the same problem commit themselves differently, just as it is not surprising that some people adopt a religion or a political cause and others in the same position do not.

These ways of being a non-rationalist about ethical judgment are not mutually exclusive. A non-rationalist could believe that some judgments follow from an ideology, some arise from emotional response, and some are existential commitments. Whatever their genesis, they are supposed to be fundamentally non-rational, and their explanation, if they have one, is a matter for psychology or sociology. Non-rationalists believe that disagreements about morality are not real disagreements, epistemologically speaking, and that there is usually no answer to the question, which judgment is right? For this reason, they face a credibility problem. Their view is at odds with the way we normally understand our moral judgments – with what I have called the view from the inside. An individual does not take his moral judgments to be an expression of feeling or a matter of personal commitment. He does not regard a moral point of view as conventional, in the way that rules of etiquette are conventional. Conscientious individuals are inclined to think that their beliefs are rationally grounded, and that what they think is right *is* right. They can be persuaded that they are mistaken or that something is wrong with their moral sensibility, but they will continue to believe that it is *possible* to judge rightly even when they have doubts about their own ability to do so. Furthermore, the idea that moral judgments depend on personal or ideological motivations or commitments is at odds with the kind of authority which moral judgments are assumed to possess. Individuals are not supposed to be judging merely for themselves. Even Sartre insists that in making an ethical decision an individual is not merely deciding for himself but for the whole of humankind (a remark which suggests that it may be wrong to attribute a non-rationalist view to him).[3]

The belief that ethical judgments are rational and objective deeply affects the way most of us think about right or wrong. But we could be in error. Non-rationalists can be interpreted as sceptics about the presumptions of the inside view. They are saying that we *think* that our ethical judgments are rational and right, or a least that they can become so, but in reality there is no such thing as a rational, authoritative ethical judgment. Our common assumptions of what we are accomplishing, or aiming for, when we judge and reason about ethical matters are simply mistaken.

Some philosophers think that the question of whether non-rationalists are right about ethical judgment hangs on the truth or falsity of realist theories of value. If values are in the world, if they are objective in this sense, then it is reasonable to suppose that our judgments about them can also be as rational as empirical judgments (though a sceptic could still insist that it is impossible for us to know what values are in the world). If values are created by valuers, then the most plausible position, according to Harman, is ' . . . a moral relativism that says that different agents are subject to different basic moral requirements depending on the moral conventions in which they participate' (Harman 1984: 30). However, the view that values are created by valuers does not preclude a rational and universal ethics (for instance one founded on a theory about what human beings are or what they need). Even if relativism is right – if individuals of different cultures are likely to end up with different values – this does not entail that they cannot be rational about what they value (or that they are not able to criticise their traditional values). The crucial issue in arguments against non-rationalists about moral rationality is not whether values are real but whether and how they are justified. An ontological stand, at least by itself, does not determine whether scepticism about ethical rationality is right or wrong, plausible or implausible. What is required is an epistemological investigation.

This means that we need to determine why individuals think that their judgments are rational and right and whether they are justified in doing so. The ethical decision-procedures I examined in Chapter 1 were supposed to do the job of explicating our moral reasoning and showing why it is rational. These procedures, particularly the more sophisticated models of Rawls and Daniels, do succeed in demonstrating that some versions of non-rationalism are wrong. Ethical judgment does not rest on either principles or intuitions which cannot be further justified or called into question. By rejecting foundationalism Rawls, Daniels and others are combating the idea that ethical reasoning is founded on assumptions which have no rational basis (though that doesn't mean that they think that all foundationalists are non-rationalists). However, since their models do not give us reason to believe that disagreement can be transcended, they leave room for non-rationalists to claim that non-rational factors are responsible for the variations in judgment and interpretation among those who use the same method.

Another way of explaining this failure of method to achieve consensus, the one I will defend, is that standard procedures, modelled as they are on the method of the sciences, do not tell us the full story of how to make judgments about moral matters. By trying to leave out or transcend everything personal they leave us in the dark about why individuals judge differently, and they provide no way of coping with difference. The idea that it is a mistake to model ethics on science or insist that ethical reasoning be impersonal is not new. Iris Marion Young and others have rejected the ideal of impartiality and insist that ethical reasoning is 'situated'. What we need to know is exactly what this means.

Moral perspectives: Gilligan and beyond

I suggested in Chapter 1 that agents who find themselves in disagreement are approaching moral problems from a different perspective. If the non-foundationalist account of ethical reasoning is right, then this must be something different from holding different basic principles or having different fundamental intuitions. A more sophisticated and useful explanation of some forms of ethical dissonance is provided by the moral psychologist, Carol Gilligan. Though her account of ethical perspective has been variously interpreted and requires amendment, it puts us on the right path in our search for an explanation of difference.

Gilligan argues, on the basis of data she collected from interviews and psychological testing, that many women have a different 'orientation' from men to moral problem solving. Men are inclined, in her view, to reason from standards of justice. They begin by determining what are the obligations and rights of the individuals concerned, and judge accordingly. Women are more inclined to consider how actions are likely to affect relationships among individuals or satisfy their needs. One of her well-known examples of difference in orientation is her contrast between a boy who thinks it obvious that a man whose wife's life is threatened should steal the drug that can save her if the druggist refuses to sell it to him at a price he can afford, and a girl's much more ambivalent and agonised approach to the same problem: her worries about what consequences stealing the drug would have for the relationships between the man and the druggist or the man and his wife (Gilligan 1982: 26ff.).

I am not here concerned with the thesis which especially interests some feminists – that women think differently about moral problems from men – but about Gilligan's use of 'orientation' to account for moral difference. Difference of orientation, she obviously thinks, cannot properly be understood as a difference in moral premises or intuitions about particular cases. It cannot be adequately represented as a higher level assumption in the procedure of finding a wide reflective equilibrium. An orientation, as she describes it, is better understood as a way of perceiving which affects every aspect of moral reasoning: what individuals regard as moral problems, how they see and describe the states of affairs which call for judgment, how they generalise and apply their generalisations, what background information they regard as relevant, and how they use it. Gilligan compares differences in orientation to the ways in which people are inclined to see an ambiguous figure in a Gestalt experiment (like the figure that can be interpreted from one point of view as an old woman and from the other as a young woman) (Gilligan 1987: 19ff.). A moral orientation, as she describes it, is more global and less easy to manipulate. It is closely tied to an individual's identity and personal development. It is not merely a way of seeing but a way of being in the world, of carrying on relations between oneself and others.

However, Gilligan and her followers are not of one mind about what it is to have an orientation. Sometimes they regard an orientation as I have described it: as a way of interpreting moral states of affairs and generalising from them. This suggests that agents with different orientations may reason in accordance with the model provided by Rawls or Daniels but don't reach the same conclusions because they describe the facts of the matter differently, have different ideas about what is morally important or what information is relevant. They share a conception of reason, but live in different moral universes. However, Gilligan and her interpreters commonly claim that those who have different orientations *reason* differently about moral matters. Those who take the justice approach, she says, subsume particular cases under general principles and deduce conclusions from these generalisations. (Gilligan thinks it symptomatic that a boy in one of Kohlberg's groups said that solving a moral problem is like doing a maths problem.) Those with the care perspective, on the other hand, focus on particulars: the complexities of the case at hand, the particular relations and needs of the people concerned. Lawrence Blum says that for those with the care perspective 'moral action itself involves an irreducible particularity – a particularity of the agent, the other and the situation' (Blum 1988: 475). Nel Noddings thinks that by abstracting from particular situations in order to formulate moral principles 'we often lose the very qualities or factors that gave rise to the moral question in the situation' (Noddings 1984: 85). Seyla Benhabib claims that justice reasoning treats individuals abstractly while care reasoning treats them as concrete persons (Benhabib 1992: 159). Men's reasoning, according to these interpretations, is mapped by the decision-procedures of moral theory. Women's reasoning is not captured by these models.

However, Gilligan's data give us no reason to think that the care and justice orientations amount to fundamental differences in ways of reasoning.[4] Attempts to present them as different rationalities go wrong, first of all, because they depend upon a caricature of 'justice reasoning'.

They assume that it involves a rigid application of rules and an insensitivity to features of a case which can make the rules problematic. Second, they depend on a confusion between rational method and style of reasoning. Style is affected by interest. Moral theorists, because of what they are aiming for, are likely to emphasise principles and their justification; moral agents who face a difficult choice are more likely to concentrate on becoming clear about the features of the case. Styles of reasoning can also differ among individuals. Some moral reasoners are inclined to refer to principles in their reasoning; others never mention such things, but are content to justify their conclusions by reference to similarities with other cases. Nevertheless, comparison depends upon seeing cases as alike, and thus on generalisations, however implicit. One question at issue between moral agents is how abstract – how extensive and inclusive – generalisations should be. However, this dispute doesn't amount to a difference in rationality. There is no reason to suppose that different styles of moral reasoning cannot all be accommodated by the method provided by Rawls or Daniels.

So we return to the idea that difference in orientation puts individuals into different moral worlds as far as interpretation and judgment are concerned. Ethical disagreement exists, according to this conception because the gap between orientations is unbridgeable – at least by any rational means. However, this idea of difference gives rise to a familiar dilemma about what being rational is supposed to require. Either the ethical judgments made by individuals with different orientations are rationally justified (according to the same criteria of rationality) or they are not. If they are rational, the argument goes, then there should be a rational means of bringing them together in a judgment that is more objective, closer to the truth, than any one of them. For if we believe that individuals who judge differently are as rational as we are, then we should want to understand their judgments, take them into account and incorporate their insights into our own view. Otherwise we will not have taken into account everything that is relevant to the determination of truth. Gilligan sometimes suggests that an adequate account of our social responsibilities requires a dialogue between justice and care (1982: 174). On the other hand, the argument continues, if moral orientations are simply the result of individual idiosyncrasies or contingencies of personality development, then the non-rationalist view of moral judgment is vindicated. Gilligan's comparison of orientations with ways of perceiving ambiguous figures seems to provide support for the non-rationalist view. For how an individual interprets a Gestalt figure probably has to do with non-rational factors of personality and situation.

The dilemma presupposes that if a way of perceiving counts as rational, then differences of opinion resulting from orientation must be rationally resolvable. From a monological point of view this means that it must be possible for a rational individual to incorporate them into a point of view which transcends their differences. This is a requirement we are naturally inclined to accept when we view ethical judgments from what I call the inside perspective. We want to think that an epistemological agent can, at least in principle, reconcile all rational points of view into a single, coherent picture of the world, empirical or ethical. However, there is no a priori reason to believe that this can always be done, and the persistence of apparently irreconcilable ethical points of view suggests that there is something wrong with this assumption, at least when it is applied to ethics. The question remains, how can we understand orientations as rational ways of approaching ethical problems and yet, as far as their proponents are concerned, irreconcilably different?

Owen Flanagan's critical examination of Gilligan's interpretation of her data suggests a way in which this question can be answered. Flanagan argues that Gilligan's Gestalt analogy creates a false picture of what an orientation is. It suggests that there are just two ways of perceiving moral situations and that an individual, because of brute facts about his personality or upbringing, is bound to perceive in either one way or the other, and that those who perceive in one of these ways will see exactly the same thing. Flanagan claims that all of these assumptions are wrong. There is no reason, he says, for thinking that other orientations are not possible: orientations guided by such things as a commitment to personal integrity, liberation, moderation, etc. (Flanagan 1991: 209). Neither are orientations discrete, autonomous ways of seeing. Both women and men adapt their way of seeing and change from one orientation to another as the situation demands. Moreover, individuals seem to be able to combine perspectives, and mix them in various ways, emphasising sometimes one way of seeing, but not abandoning the other.

> It seems more plausible to think that particular judgments, actions and personalities (imagine a merciful judge or a loving and fair parent) express a complex set of moral concerns and dispositions rather than that they express first one voice and then another or that they express two distinct voices at once.
>
> (Flanagan 1991: 209)

Orientations or perspectives are not set scripts which individuals adopt as the result of deep psychological differences or upbringing, but are ways in which they creatively respond to the vicissitudes of their lives; and the bringing together of perspectives is not only something that can be done, but an activity which requires reason, reflection and experience. However, individuals have their own way of interpreting their values and reconciling them in their lives. There is not just one way of being a just or caring person, or reconciling justice and care.

An orientation or a perspective, his discussion suggests, is an individual's way of identifying and interpreting moral states of affairs integrated by an idea or ideas of what is morally important – whether this is justice, care, courage, integrity, etc., or some combination of these. A perspective, so understood, is, or can be, a creative response to the living of a life – to the experiences of an individual, his roles and relationships, and his reflections on what they mean. This means that having an orientation is not a brute fact about an individual or the legacy of unconscious forces over which he has no control. Nor is a perspective beyond the reach of criticism. It can be refined and altered as an individual encounters problems, has new experiences, listens to the criticisms of others or reflects on his life. A person can come to realise that his perspective is naive, or inadequate for the solution of some kinds of problems, or that it makes him insensitive towards certain kinds of people or situations, or that it sometimes distorts his vision. He can alter and improve it. A perspective is as much the fruit of experience and reflection as the basis for it.

The nature of moral perception

Flanagan provides us with a way of understanding a moral orientation or perspective as a rational way of perceiving and guiding moral behaviour: as an integrated system of values, propensities, beliefs and perceptions which is the product of a person's situation and life experiences, and his reflection on these experiences. Flanagan's account shows that moral views, and the orientation they depend on, can be rational without this presupposing the existence of a transcendent perspective from which all orientations can be criticised and judged. An individual will often want to comprehend and take into account the points of view of others. The ways in which other people approach moral problems can be a source of inspiration, or they can challenge aspects of our own ways of acting and judging. Nevertheless, how a person assesses and makes use of the views of others will depend upon *his* orientation. This explains why he can take into account the views of others and still reach different conclusions from theirs. A moral orientation is part of an individual's personality. It is rational, but at the same time personal in the sense that it is a perspective that he has developed for himself and it is not necessarily shared by others.

A critic might complain that this conception of an orientation doesn't make sense: that it leads back to a version of the dilemma about rationality. If an orientation counts as rational then it seems it must be assessable from an impartial, impersonal standpoint. If it cannot be so assessed (if there is no impersonal standpoint), then it must be, at bottom, non-rational. However the idea of rationality implicit in this objection is implausibly severe. All of our knowledge, empirical as well as ethical, depends upon a way of comprehending experiences which cannot be justified by reference to some higher framework. Empirical knowledge depends upon our being able to perceive and interpret our perceptions. This does not mean that our empirical perceptions are brute, uncriticisable facts. Perception can be criticised, refined and trained; we can make discoveries which require us to change our way of seeing. Our way of perceiving is thus both the basis for theory and the consequence of it. The perceptual basis of empirical knowledge is as rational as the judgments which depend on it (indeed, we could not regard these judgments as fully rational if we did not assume this). Nevertheless, to assess the evidence for theories which challenge some of our perceptual assumptions we have to be able to interpret our perceptions. We always have to have a perspective in order to make judgments about the world (even though this perspective is itself subject to refinement and revision). There is no higher court of appeal to which we can bring questions about rationality, and for this reason sceptical doubts about our ability to know are always possible. However, this is a possibility of doubt which we are forced to live with, since we do not have any option but to judge and act on the basis of our beliefs about the world.

The perspective which enables an individual to make moral judgments is, I suggest, analogous to the perceptual perspective from which he makes judgments about the empirical world. The fact that ethical judgment, including judgment about judgments, always takes place from a perspective, is no more a reason for questioning ethical rationality than the fact that empirical judgments, however sophisticated and critical, always depend upon a way of perceiving. The nature of ethical judgments and how they are justified give us no *special* reason to be sceptics about ethical rationality.

However, there is clearly a crucial difference between empirical and ethical judgments. In the empirical case, we can usually assume that individuals who are properly trained and attentive will respond in the same way to the data of experience. It so happens that the world is such, and human perception is such, that individuals from their various points of view can generally manage to converge in their perceptual judgments. A happy outcome to the fable of the elephant depends on this being so. Science, it could be said, has deliberately and systematically confined itself to areas of investigation where individuals, after appropriate training, can reliably reach distributive agreement, at least about basic data. The primary/secondary quality distinction, along with a preference for properties that can be quantified, have played an important role in its selection of subject matter. Science is determinedly monological and can get away with it; ethics cannot. However conscientiously and thoroughly he reasons, an ethical agent cannot transcend *his* assessment of the data of experience, *his* view of the criticisms of others, *his* way of reflecting. An ethics that tried to imitate science by insisting on conformity would be a perversion. People can be forced into ethical agreement by indoctrination, threats or the discouragement of criticism. But this method of achieving consensus depends upon suppression of individuals' attempts to be conscientious and rational. It has no relation to the kind of training which makes scientists into agents capable of reaching consensus.

Looking at the matter in this way, it appears that the assumption basic to the dilemma about rationality is an attempt to impose upon us requirements which are reasonable for science but not for ethics. We can reasonably assume that empirical disagreements among rational agents can and should be monologically resolved by a position which incorporates what is right about each view (or shows that one or more is mistaken). However, we cannot assume that this is possible for every form of rational inquiry. We have good reason to think that it is not generally possible for ethics, at least by monological means. This does not mean that ethical judgments are not as rational as empirical judgments. On the other hand, if the dilemma about rationality is interpreted as imposing on empirical and ethical inquiry the requirement that all judgments and ways of interpreting must be justified by reference to an indubitable standpoint, then this ideal of rationality cannot be satisfied by either form of inquiry.

It might be objected that the claim that moral perception is no less sound a basis for rational judgment than is empirical perception, has not been established. Not all empirical perceptions are equal. Some are not a reliable basis for making judgments. Not everyone sees colours in the same way. Some people are colour blind: what others see as blue or red, orange or yellow, they perceive as muddy brown. Objects under certain conditions (for example in ultraviolet light) appear to have different colours than they do under normal circumstances. Because people see colours differently or see them differently under different conditions, they cannot always regard their colour perceptions as a reason for thinking that the world is as it appears to them. It might be argued that moral perception is more like colour perception than it is like the perceptions that scientists rely on when they construct their theories, and that differences of moral perception are rather like differences of colour perception. Just as the colour blind person, or the person in a room lit by ultraviolet light, is not entitled to regard his perceptions, however clear and distinct, as a rational basis for making judgments about the world, so too the ethical judge is not entitled to regard his perceptions as a rational basis for making judgments about what is right.

The problem with this analogy is that we do have reason to regard some perceptions of colour under some conditions as right. They are the ones which enable us to make important discriminations in the circumstances that usually obtain. As the term suggests, people who are 'colour blind' are not perceiving the world rightly. They are liable to make unfortunate mistakes at traffic lights; they cannot fully appreciate a Van Gogh painting. Their equivalent in the moral case would not be individuals who have a different, maybe less common, orientation, but an individual who is 'blind' to certain kinds of people or considerations – say, the comfortable white middle class person who simply cannot comprehend the point of view of a poor black single mother (though in this case, the blindness may be curable).

Let us suppose that about half the population tastes a particular substance as sour and the other half tastes it as sweet. Each can make the same discriminations, and so there is no reason to regard one way of perceiving as right or normal and the other as wrong or abnormal. On the other hand, we would probably not want to say that either way of perceiving provides individuals with a reason for judging that something in the world is really sour or is really sweet. Such differences in taste seem best understood as merely subjective responses to something in the world, the result, perhaps, of a genetic quirk. If differences in moral perception are like these differences in taste, then the claim that orientations are rational, and that the judgments that depend on them should be taken seriously as claims about right, seem ill-founded.

There is an obvious disanalogy between differences in perceptions of taste and differences in moral perception. That people taste something differently is a brute fact about them unconnected with any of their other perceptions or judgments. This is one of the reasons why we are inclined to think that the way they perceive is merely a subjective quirk. Moral perceptions, on the contrary, are part of a system of judgment, perception and reflection which can be adjusted and refined on the basis of experience and criticism.

However, suppose that in the imagined population the taste perceptions of individuals differ in a systematic way over a wide range of substances. In each group individuals can refine and classify their perceptions; they develop a vocabulary to describe what they perceive, make value judgments about what tastes are superior, develop and refine a cuisine which presents subtle variations of the tastes they favour as well as providing new experiences for them to classify, discuss and evaluate. There are, so to speak, two different universes of taste. What tastes good to people in one universe does not taste good to those in the other, and the subtle refinements and interesting combinations that the gourmets in one group enthuse about are not appreciated by those in the other. Try as they might, they cannot learn to like what the other group eats. They always go to different restaurants. The example is now much more similar to the case of moral difference. Moreover, I think we would be much more inclined to say that these differences of taste perception are not mere subjective quirks: that the judgments made by members of each group and their systems of perceptions and evaluations deserve to be regarded as rational.

There remains an important distinction between the imagined case of perceptual difference and the differences that exist between moral orientations. We reasonably suppose that differences in perceptions of taste, however much these perceptions are later refined by experience or subjected to critical evaluation, are primarily due to some feature of an individual's sense organs or nervous system. They are in this sense arbitrary. This is another reason why we are inclined to think that an individual's judgments about taste are a subjective response to the world and for this reason rational only 'up to a point'. Though an individual's psychic constitution undoubtedly affects his moral outlook, his judgments, particularly after they have been subjected to criticism and the lessons of experience, cannot so easily be attributed to personal idiosyncrasies. As Flanagan suggests, moral difference is often more closely attributable to environmental factors like the social relations in which individuals are embedded, the experiences they happen to have, or the roles that they are expected to play.

However, the difference is not merely that taste perceptions are likely to be the result of inner causes and moral perceptions are more likely to be the result of outer influences. A parent who has learned to perceive and respond in a caring way to those for whom he is responsible does not do what he does because his social role or some other environmental factors determine him to perceive and act in a particular way. An intrinsic part of his moral orientation is the considered belief that his role is a valuable one, that the experiences which influenced his judgments provide him with insights; that his social environment, or aspects of it, have had a positive role in forming his moral point of view. This does not mean that individuals cannot be critical of their social roles or their social environment. However, the crucial point is that the factors which influence our moral judgments are not mere causes but are themselves things that we evaluate and sometimes have reason to value.

This means, first of all, that we have stronger reasons for thinking that our moral perspective, and the moral judgments that depend on it, are rational, than we have for thinking judgments about taste are rational in the case I imagined. Second, it explains why we are sometimes entitled to think that the personal and environmental factors which form our orientation are not merely causes of diversity, but are sources of insight. To be a parent, to experience hardship, to grow up in a frugal middle class family, to be acquainted with people of different ethnic backgrounds, and other such factors which help to shape a moral point of view, are often recognised by those who reflect on their moral lives as providing them with an outlook or sensitivity which contributes to their ability to make good moral judgments. However, this difference between moral judgments and the imagined perceptual judgments means that moral judgments pose a special problem.

People who make different judgments about taste are, apparently, saying contradictory things about the world. Nothing can be both sweet and sour, etc. This is clearly a problem, but one we think that we can solve by looking for an explanation of why the world appears to each group in the way it does: a scientific, and therefore universally acceptable, reason for the difference. If we find that the difference can be explained as the result of a genetic factor which causes taste buds to develop in different ways, then the problem has been solved. We might not want to conclude that what individuals perceive is the mere appearance of an underlying reality, for this suggests that tastes are only subjective. The fact remains that tastes are for these individuals an important part of their world, the object of intersubjective experience and discussion. We might allow for this by saying that their 'reality' or their conception of world is different in some respects. Taste, we might conclude, is a relative matter. This means that there is no point in asking whose judgments are true. The judgments of both groups can be regarded as true relative to their particular way of being in the world. Presumably individuals, once they are apprised of the facts, will have no trouble agreeing that this is so.

The case is different for moral orientations. Individuals, at least when they take the inside perspective, do not accept the idea that their views are only relatively true. They think that those who have a different moral point of view are wrong, and they insist on continuing the moral debate. Given the nature of moral judgment, this is not surprising. For a moral perspective owes its existence not to a psychic quirk but to experiences, social influences or ways of living which individuals have reason to regard as the source of moral insights. The statements individuals make about tastes are rational and right relative to a way of perceiving which has to be regarded as given. The moral judgments individuals make are rational and right relative to a way of seeing which is itself perceived to have moral value. So it is reasonable for individuals to regard their moral views as rational 'all the way down' and not accept the idea that they are merely true relative to a particular framework.

An individual's belief that his ethical judgments are not merely rational relative to a way of perceiving, but that his way of perceiving is itself morally valuable, will affect the way in which he regards the judgments of those he disagrees with. If these others are also rational, if there is no reason to think that they are prejudiced, insensitive or reasoning badly, then he has reason to think that they are also arguing from a view which is morally valuable. As a conscientious, rational moral agent he will want to understand this view and incorporate it into his own. Indeed as a rational individual he must want to do this. For once he recognises that others can have moral insights that he does not possess, that the conclusions they reach as the fruits of their experiences and reflections, could be relevant to his own judgments, then he will have to regard his own views and his own perspective as partial – as epistemologically incomplete.

An agent has good reason for wanting to comprehend and take into account the views of other rational agents. However, what the agent wants to obtain – a transcendent judgment which incorporates the views of others – is impossible for him to achieve. For he will inevitably assess and take into account the views of others from his own perspective. (How else could he do this?) And thus he is likely, at least sometimes, to reach different conclusions from other equally conscientious individuals who are also taking into account the views of others (including himself).

Ethical judgments are rational, but are made from different perspectives. They are in this respect 'personal'. They are also limited because a perspective is limited. There exist legitimate and indeed insightful ways of perceiving and understanding possessed by those who have other perspectives. Being situated means being limited and partial. But being partial is not a condition with which an individual should be content. An individual has good reason for wanting to overcome his partiality. This is why he thinks he must aim for transcendence: for a higher level perspective from which he can judge all ethical positions. However, there is good reason to think that this transcendent perspective is not available to him. We are not able to give an account of how an individual can judge impersonally and impartially even in principle.

The account of moral judgment I am presenting provides an explanation for some kinds of persistent disagreement, but at the same time a defence of the conviction that our moral beliefs can be as well-supported by evidence and argument as our empirical beliefs. This investigation thus provides a defence of the conviction that our ethical views are, or can be, rational. Not merely rational given a set of unjustifiable assumptions or an arbitrarily determined way of perceiving, but as fully rational as a view can be. They are what I will call 'cogent'. To this extent the inside view of moral judgment is vindicated. On the other hand, the investigation does not support the other assumption that we are inclined to make when we adopt the inside view: that our cogent judgments are right or true, and that other rational individuals ought to accept them.

A conscientious ethical agent who has taken into account the criticisms and opinions of others is disposed to believe that his view is right, not just because it is the result of impeccable reasoning, but because he thinks he has taken into account the views of others and made an impartial assessment of them. He thinks his judgment is objective because it *seems* to him that he has transcended the merely personal, and has arrived at a conclusion that should be accepted by all rational agents. What an investigation into the nature of ethical judgment reveals is that the inside view of ethical judgment is, in this respect, seriously mistaken, and an individual's claim to ethical authority cannot be upheld. An individual's ethical reasoning, properly appreciated, is not capable of being impartial. It is not capable of achieving the kind of objectivity that would entitle him to make such a claim.

The position we have reached is not a comfortable one from either a moral or an epistemological point of view. The view that individuals can make impersonal, impartial judgments about what is right is mistaken. However, non-rationalism is also false. And since we have good reason for thinking that good moral judgment requires us to take into account the ethical views of others, relativism is also unattractive. It seems that we ought to strive for transcendence but cannot achieve it. This is a predicament, and we obviously cannot be satisfied with leaving the matter as it is.

The answer to this predicament that I am going to argue for is ethical collectivism: a thesis which offers a way of bridging the gap between what rationality requires and what individual agents are capable of doing, a way of overcoming the limitations of individual judgment, resolving the tension between inside and outside views of ethical judgment, and underwriting the authority of ethical judgment. According to ethical collectivists, impartiality and right judgment is achieved, not by an act of individual transcendence, but through a collective procedure in which a conclusion is constructed out of the insightful positions of individuals.

However, to many people a collectivist solution to the problem is going to seem too radical. They may prefer to think that ethical relativism is more likely to be right. If an individual can't be impartial, they are likely to argue, then the more plausible conclusion is that there is no such thing as impartiality. If all our efforts to understand and take into account the positions of others do not lead to consensus, then perhaps the objective is not a sensible one. After all, the inside view of our ethical judgments has to be revised, and relativism provides a well-known suggestion about how to do it. By looking more closely at the reasons for rejecting relativism the motivation for adopting ethical collectivism will become stronger.

Radical relativism

There is a well-worn path from the realisation that individuals cannot legislate for others to a radical relativist position on ethical judgment. An individual can morally legislate, according to the radical relativist, but only for himself. His moral beliefs can be called true, but they are only true for him. He can claim no authority over the decisions and actions of others, and his disagreements with others are merely apparent. The account of ethical judgment I advocate seems to provide support for this position. Ethical inquiry, according to the non-foundationalist view of ethical rationality, is a voyage on a Neurathian ship: a vessel which has to be repaired under sail. The personal nature of ethical judgment suggests that we are all bobbing around in our individual boats.

Radical relativism is not radical enough. It assumes that individuals can make authoritative judgments for themselves, if not for others – but this is often not so. For those who retreat to the self and its convictions find no refuge from ethical dissonance. The differences of ethical opinion that divide individuals can sometimes occur within the mind of a single agent. Agents can fail to solve a moral problem, not because they are baffled about what a solution would be, but because they are in two minds (or more) about how to solve it. It is not difficult to understand how this can happen. Individuals play a number of roles in their social lives and develop different kinds of relationships. They do not have just one situation. These relationships and roles are associated with particular obligations and expectations; they are the source of experience, the subject of moral reflection, and encourage individuals to learn how to interpret and appraise in a particular way. However, roles and relationships can come into conflict, and ethical questions can arise to which an individual from his different situations is inclined to give inconsistent answers. He is not necessarily going to be able to resolve all of his ethical quandaries by discovering a satisfactory way to make the demands of his perspectives compatible or a good reason for subordinating one of his values to the other.

Some philosophers think that only a deontologist is in danger of encountering a case where his moral principles give him contradictory guidance, and that consequentialists, since they only have one moral principle, escape this difficulty. However, the problem I am concerned with is not the same as that usually discussed under the heading 'ethical dilemmas': the predicament of having principles which make contradictory demands. Internal dissonance occurs because agents can have more than one perspective, or a number of ways of interpreting a perspective, and are thus not always one with themselves in their interpretation of individual cases, or in their application of a principle or conception of what background information is important. Those who are inclined to judge in a consequentialist way will be as subject to such quandaries as are deontologists.

If a person is at odds with himself, his attempts to be rational and objective will not always solve the problem. When he takes up one of his points of view and reasons from it, he reaches a conclusion which seems to him to be the best possible conclusion. When he is under the influence of another perspective he reaches a contrary conclusion which seems to him to be as well-supported as an ethical conclusion can be. The predicament of Sartre's student (1975: 354), who had to decide between staying with his mother and joining the Free French, might be understood in this way: that is, we might interpret his difficulty as resulting from a clash between perspectives. When he thinks as a son, a member of a family who has intimate relations with others, he reaches the conclusion that these relations are of great moral importance and must take priority in any conflict of interests. On the other hand, he is also a citizen, a public person, who is supposed to have wider responsibilities (assuming that his reflections on justice lead him to that conclusion).[5] From this point of view it seems clear that personal relationships and the responsibilities associated with them sometimes have to be sacrificed for the sake of justice or the greater good. The student may not be able to decide what to do because each of these ways of looking at the situation seem equally rational, the conclusions reached from the perspective of each equally weighty, and further reflection does not give him any reason to think that one is better than the other. If an individual is in this kind of predicament, then what he faces is not merely the question of how to make a particular decision, but a more general problem of how to reconcile perspectives, each of which seems to be equally well-supported by experience and reflection. How he does this is going to affect other decisions that he makes and therefore how he develops as a moral person.

If an individual, even a radical relativist, does not always know how to determine what is true for himself, disagreement once again poses an epistemological problem. The relativist might deal with this problem by subscribing to a thesis which is even more radical than radical relativism. The 'really radical relativist' holds that the judgment a person is predisposed to make now, or in this situation, is correct for him as the person who is in his present situation. The judgment that he makes in another situation under the influence of another perspective is correct for him as the person in that situation. We can give this thesis a postmodernist rationale. There is no such thing as an essential or unitary self. An individual has many situations and thus many selves – each of which has its own way of judging, acting and interpreting. Since we have more than one moral personality, we can interpret and evaluate our actions and lives, and the actions and lives of others, in many ways, and there is no reason to think that one interpretation is better than another. The demand for self-consistency is an imposition, a form of oppression, which we are justified in resisting.

The problem is, obviously, that however many selves an individual may have, he has only one body, only one life. The student must decide to do one thing or the other. Should he decide the matter by flipping a coin? From a really radical relativist point of view this seems like the only way he can make up his mind. The problem with resolving the matter in this way is that it doesn't do justice to his perspectives or the way in which the conclusions derived from them are justified. First of all, this is because each of his positions is rational. Each is well-supported by perception and critical reflection. Each, he has reason to believe, is an insightful moral opinion. To dismiss one of his positions by the flip of coin is a flippant way to treat a moral insight.

The second, related reason why an agent needs a non-arbitrary way of making up his mind is because he has grounds for believing that each of his perspectives is limited and partial. A radical relativist, or a really radical relativist, has to suppose that the view of an individual, or an individual-in-a-situation, is complete and satisfactory as it is. A person's judgment is the measure of his own moral universe (or that of the moral universe he shares with others). But when we think about what makes moral judgment possible, or why moral conundrums occur, we recognise that this idea is not attractive. Judgment depends on situation, and having a situation is limiting. The young man knows that it is not adequate to approach his problem merely from the perspective of a family member or merely from the perspective of a public person. As a conscientious person he has to acknowledge that judging from the standpoint of one of his situations does not enable him to encompass the insights available from another. The fact that each of these perspectives is not the whole story is one reason why making a decision is so difficult, and why an arbitrary resolution will not do.

This is not merely a problem for really radical relativism. Once we recognise that ethical judgment is limited, then the radical relativist position itself becomes unattractive. By insisting that an individual can regard as true what he believes to be true, it fails to take into account everything we know about ethical judgment. For if we know our own judgments are limited, then how can we in good faith declare them to be true even for ourselves? A radical relativist, it seems, must be a non-rationalist. He must assume that making up our minds about an ethical problem is an arbitrary act, and thus it doesn't matter how it is done. However, there are good reasons for thinking that non-rationalism is wrong.

What Sartre's student, or anyone else who faces a moral predicament, should want is a solution which gives each of his well-founded but limited points of view equal weight (since each of them seems to him equally weighty). The rational way to accomplish this, and what most agents probably do, is to try to step outside both of the perspectives and determine, as an independent arbiter might, a way of solving the problem that gives each position its due. This does not necessarily mean finding a 'compromise' solution to a particular problem. The student either leaves his mother or he does not; a woman either has an abortion or she does not. What these individuals want is not merely an answer to a particular problem. Their internal conflict is a symptom of a more general difficulty. They want a way of combining and balancing their perspectives so that they can obtain a rational and principled stance towards a number of related problems. They want guidelines for negotiating between the demands morality makes upon them. If he is successful in reconciling his perspectives, the young man will determine how to balance his private and public duties; he will have guidelines enabling him to do this, and as a result will now know how to think about the problem at hand. Even though he may still feel torn between conflicting duties, regretting that he cannot fulfil both, at least he will know what he should do. The position he reaches will not necessarily be in accordance with the feelings or intuitions that he has when he looked at the problem from either of his points of view. He has stepped outside a framework that can be directly justified by either of his perspectives. Since each of these points of view have been taken into account in his construction of a position and the guidelines that follow from it, he has reason to believe that they are justified from a moral point of view – at least until some better resolution comes along.

Really radical relativism is unsatisfactory because it doesn't do justice to the nature of ethical judgment and the disagreements an individual can have with himself. The best way of dealing with this kind of conundrum, I have suggested, is to construct a proposal for reconciling perspectives, which gives each an equal weight. If this is the right way of criticising and going beyond the really radical relativist position, then, for similar reasons, it is also the right way of dealing with radical relativism. For an individual knows that his perspective (or perspectives), even when rationally well-founded, are inevitably partial. They are the result of his situation. He knows that others are, or can be, as rational as he is, and that their judgments are also limited by their situation. Once again, it seems reasonable to suppose that the rational resolution of disagreements must come from outside of the perspectives of the individuals: that it must consist of guidelines capable of taking into account and giving due weight to the positions that arise from these individual points of view. Our desire to transcend the personal and make our judgments truly impartial is a reasonable one, given their nature and limitations. The fact remains that there is no individual (at least no creature like us) who can reliably construct such a transcendent point of view. So if transcendence is possible at all, then it will have to be achieved collectively through the participation of individuals who have different situations and hold different perspectives; and they will have to go about it in a different way from the way they went about obtaining their individual judgments. The reason for rejecting radical relativism is thus a reason for becoming an ethical collectivist.

Ethical collectivism offers a way of defending our inside view of ethical judgment from both non-rationalism and radical relativism. It can do this only by bringing into question some of the assumptions we are inclined to make when we view our ethical judgments from the inside – above all, that the conscientious, rational agent is entitled to believe his judgment is *right*, or at least right for himself. The reconciliation of the inside and outside views of ethical judgment proposed by ethical collectivism requires us to acknowledge that we have, from the inside, a mistaken idea about what our ethical reasoning can accomplish, and thus about the nature and authority of our own judgments. On the other hand, it allows us to regard our own judgments as making an essential contribution to determining what is right and true. Ethical collectivism shows how we can appreciate the insights, but recognise the limitations, of individual points of view – and transcend them. This transcendence is not something that an individual can accomplish for himself by monological methods. Transcendence of the personal requires that we also transcend monological reasoning. It requires a different approach to ethical rationality.

Ethical collectivism claims that a truly rational and impersonal view can only be obtained by giving all the rational but limited views of individuals equal weight in a construction that incorporates aspects of all of them. Critics will doubt whether this can be done, or whether the results, if there are any, will be acceptable. How can an individual be expected to reach a compromise with those whose opinions he despises – and not regard it as a mere compromise for political purposes but as a view better than his own? Why should a secular humanist believe that the cause of truth will be served by reaching an accommodation with a fundamentalist Christian (or vice versa)? Why should a deontologist compromise with a utilitarian? At best, it seems, ethical collectivism will provide a means by which people with the same basic values, as well as the same ideas about ethical rationality, can reach a well-motivated conclusion about what is right. However, if ethical collectivism only applies to those whose views are pretty much the same (as similar as the views of an individual's 'selves' are likely to be) then it seems it will not get far in its attempt to solve the problems associated with disagreement. To deal with this and other difficulties we need to know more about what counts as a rational perspective and how ethical collectivists are supposed to transcend the contrary positions of individuals. This is the business of Part II.

Part II

ETHICAL REASONING FROM A COLLECTIVIST POINT OF VIEW

4

REQUIREMENTS OF ETHICAL REASONING: CRITICAL DISCOURSE

Ethical collectivism is a theory about the nature of ethical knowledge and how it is obtained. If it is going to flourish then it has to show how those who satisfy its conditions and follow its rules can arrive at an answer to their ethical questions – an answer they have reason to believe is right, and not merely a political compromise or an 'overlapping consensus'. An ethical decision-procedure does not have to establish conclusions that are beyond the reach of doubt. It can allow that we are fallible. But it must then provide us with means for identifying and correcting mistakes. It must enable us to make progress towards ethical truth.

The procedure that I advocate contains three interdependent processes. The first is the means by which an individual using his or her cognitive resources arrives at a view about how cases of a certain kind ought to be judged. The second is the process of criticising, rejecting or correcting these opinions of individuals in critical discourse. In this dialogue individuals present their generalisations about the cases they have judged, and the reasons for them, to discourse, answer criticisms and criticise others, and as a result obtain a set of cogent generalisations about the moral matters in question – positions which are as good as critical examination can now make them. Cogent generalisations are positions which have survived the rigours of monological decision-procedures. They are well-supported by relevant evidence and background theories. When they arrive at cogent positions the participants in critical discourse have accomplished as much as it is possible for them to accomplish by monological means. However, critical discourse will not generally produce a moral position with which everyone (distributively) can agree. The third stage, constructive discourse, is the non-monological process of using the results of critical discourse – the cogent generalisations – to construct a general conclusion or guideline which resolves the moral problems at issue. The first two processes supply the material from which a moral conclusion is ultimately constructed. This chapter will be concerned with these first stages; Chapter 5 will focus on what makes ethical collectivism unique – the process of constructive discourse.

Varieties of moral rationality

Requirements of rationality, whether for individuals or collectives, must be standards acceptable to everyone. As far as procedural rules are concerned, ethical collectivism has to be monological: it has to anchor itself upon conditions and standards of reasoning which are shared by each and every participant in discourse. For otherwise there would be no such thing as an ethical collectivist method, and no possibility of any kind of agreement (even a collective one). I will try to show that the requirements imposed by ethical collectivism on individuals should be accepted either because they are standard conditions of rationality – requirements that all individuals do or should acknowledge whatever their ethical or metaphysical views – or because they are conditions which must be fulfilled if critical or constructive discourses are to be possible. I am assuming that those who accept the conclusions reached in the previous chapters about the problem of disagreement and nature of ethical judgment will be motivated to accept requirements which make it possible to obtain ethical knowledge through discourse.

Nevertheless, arguments for rational standards are inevitably circular: rational requirements are what rational individuals accept and individuals are rational if they accept requirements which are rational. If there are individuals who systematically follow non-standard rules of reasoning, refuse to acknowledge that they are in error, and cannot reasonably be regarded as mad or bad, then there is no argument able to establish, in a non-question-begging way, that they are being irrational. One way in which ethical relativism could be right is if there is fundamental disagreement among ethical agents about method or what counts as a justification – disagreement which makes it impossible for everyone to participate in the same critical discourse. The existence of individuals who have different ideas about rationality should not prevent us from specifying what *we* regard as rational (whoever this 'we' turns out to be). However, the enterprise of laying down rules of method would be seriously undermined if it turns out that there is as much (or nearly as much) disagreement about requirements of rationality as there is about ethical propositions.

Philosophers have presented a range of apparently contrary ideas about how ethical reasoning should proceed. Those, like Hare, who find it difficult to understand how there can be an alternative to utilitarian reasoning advocate the procedure which he outlines in *Freedom and Reason*, or something similar. Others prefer to imagine what they would decide behind a veil of ignorance, or by abstracting from a situation any feature which has to do with themselves and their interests (as Pollock recommends). Some people think they should start with the principles and ethical ideas that they already possess and criticise and refine them as they deal with problematic cases. Others insist that what is important is having the right character: that we can rely on virtuous people to make good moral judgments. Some think that ethical conclusions should be deduced from self-evident principles; some feminist critics of ethical theory think that ethical problems should be resolved by paying close attention to the details of a situation and the interests of the people concerned. These differences of opinion about how to be ethically rational seem to preclude achieving the consensus on conditions of rationality which is presupposed by any theory of ethical knowledge (and not just ethical collectivism).

However, this diversity of method may not be as much of a problem as it first appears. Some differences in method, I have suggested, are differences of style and not substance. Whether you imagine yourself behind a veil of ignorance or use Pollock's method of abstraction is not likely to affect what conclusion you reach. Whether you start your reasoning from general principles or start with a thorough examination of the case at hand reflects a difference in interest or a difference in habits of thought, but not necessarily a difference in rationality. Some suggested approaches to ethical reasoning seem to be simply inadequate, especially in the light of the reflections on moral judgment in Part I. The idea that ethical reasoning starts from self evident principles does not adequately handle ethical dissonance. It does not do justice to the outside view of ethical judgment. The belief that the right answer to an ethical problem is what the virtuous person judges is right is not compatible with the recognition that ethical judgments of individuals are limited and personal. It would be irrational for us to place our trust in what a single individual, however virtuous, thinks is right, or to suppose that the principles we think are self-evident are true.

Some differences in approach to ethical problems, like the difference between utilitarians and deontologists or the difference between those who begin with traditional morality and those who adopt a more radical approach, are generally best understood as perspectival differences – differences resulting from divergent views about what is morally important and how to live a moral life. Utilitarians (for example) think that general well-being is of supreme moral importance (however this is understood), and deontologists think that individual integrity or justice (or something else) should dominate our moral concerns. But understood in this way the disputes which arise from these different perspectives do not exhibit a difference in rationality. Utilitarians and deontologists, conservatives and radicals are part of the same moral discourse. They can understand and appreciate each other's views, argue, engage in mutual criticism; they raise difficulties for each other which have to be taken seriously. There are, it is true, utilitarians, deontologists, defenders of traditional morality, etc. who, by refusing to allow anything to count as an objection to their view, are treating their premises as unassailable standards of rationality. Because of the circularity of all attempts to justify rational requirements, there is no way of refuting a determined attempt to redefine what makes a good ethical judgment. But this kind of dogmatism, like dogmatism about other ethical matters, is ill-suited to deal with the moral judgments that most of us are accustomed to make, and in fact most of those who call themselves utilitarians or deontologists are not dogmatists.[1]

Any disagreement about method, whether dogmatic or not, is a problem for monological approaches to ethical rationality if it leads to disagreements about ethical conclusions. Monologists either have to hope that these disagreements can somehow be resolved or they have to dictate that only one approach counts as rational – against the convictions of those who see no reason why they should have to abandon their way of reasoning. Ethical collectivists can afford to be more tolerant about differences in approach to ethical problems because they regard the judgments and justifications of individuals as raw material for critical and constructive discourse. Individuals on their own are not expected to get things right, and they do not have to arrive at the same conclusion in the same way. Difference in approach can be regarded as one of the ways in which difference of perspective manifests itself. What is required by an ethical collectivist is only that the methods and approaches of ethical agents are such that they can accept each other as participants in discourse: that they can regard each other's views and criticisms as serious contributions to obtaining ethical knowledge.

What ethical collectivism has to provide, as far as individual judgment is concerned, is not a detailed decision-procedure, but the parameters within which opinion forming has to take place: general requirements which all individuals have to accept and apply if their views are going to be considered in critical discourse. The decision-procedure for ethics presented by Rawls in 'Outline of a decision procedure for ethics', elaborated by Daniels and modified in the light of Walker's criticisms (as discussed in Chapters 1 and 2) will serve well enough as a focus for a discussion of what these general requirements must be. The fact that a procedure for individual judgment which aims at impartiality and agreement does not do justice to the personal nature of individual justifications or the problem of disagreement is not a drawback when our objective is merely to specify requirements of rationality which everyone is supposed to accept.

From the point of view of ethical collectivism the virtue of an approach to individual judgment like Rawls' is that it is procedural: an acceptable generalisation is something constructed by a competent judge from judgments made in circumstances conducive to good judgment. Ethical theorists have sometimes criticised procedural specifications of what counts as a good or true judgment for being too indirect. Would we answer questions about mathematics, asks Alan Donagan, by saying what ideal calculators would do (1977: 220)? For ethical collectivists, who believe that ethics is not at all like mathematics, the lack of specific directions is an advantage. Rawls' procedure leaves it up to the individual exactly what form of reasoning she employs in order to reach her judgments. The way the agent perceives individual cases and reasons about them will be affected by her ethical point of view, and thus so will her generalisations. She is not required by the method to adopt any particular ethical theory or moral presuppositions. She is free to approach the ethical cases she judges as a utilitarian or a deontologist. She is free to judge in her own way from her own point of view, in the light of her reflections on her moral life and the lessons learned from others. She can take into account general ideas about individuals and their relationships in the way she thinks appropriate. The procedure merely requires that she satisfy conditions of competency and accept basic principles of rational argument. Individuals who count as competent will often reach different ethical conclusions. For ethical collectivists this is only to be expected and is not a problem for the procedure.

If Rawls' procedure is regarded merely as providing necessary and sufficient conditions for an individual's judgments being considered in critical discourse, then we do not have to be so concerned about how competent judges really are. Rawls rightly wants to allow that ordinary people with average intelligence and a reasonable amount of knowledge can be competent judges. This creates a difficulty if individual judgment is assumed to be as authoritative as Rawls wants it to be. For individuals, even those who are extremely intelligent, can sometimes be insensitive, stupid, narrow-minded or careless, and they can lack background knowledge which may be required for what Daniels calls 'wide reflective equilibrium'. Even self-reflection cannot be guaranteed to cure these ills. On the other hand, individuals who are of less than average intelligence or are mentally ill may have a moral view that deserves consideration. Feminist critics are rightly concerned about ethical decision-procedures which seem to favour educated, articulate and 'normal' individuals. If individual judgments are regarded merely as the input to critical discourse, then we don't have to be so concerned about just how competent an agent is or about the depth or breadth of her knowledge. Faults in individuals' reasoning can be detected and remedied in critical discourse, and they can become acquainted with information or general considerations which are relevant to their ethical conclusions. Discourse is a device for improving the competence of judges: it can overcome their ignorance, correct their errors; it can reveal untoward influences and hidden prejudices, and can take up the conclusions of a not-so-competent judge and consider whether there is anything to be said for them. It can also provide and apply the general considerations necessary for wide reflective equilibrium.

The same point can be made about Rawls' restrictions on the circumstances in which judges make judgments. Rawls' concern is that even the most competent judges have a tendency to make mistakes under certain circumstances – for example, if they are under threat or pressure, or if their own interests are at stake. On the other hand, it might be argued that those who have something at stake are more likely to be sensitive to and knowledgeable about matters which others miss. Walker thinks that moral rationality is often best exercised, not by independent judges, but by individuals who together work out an answer to their own moral problems. One of the problems for monological decision-procedures is that there seems to be no entirely right position for authoritative judgment, no situation from which such a judgment can reliably be made. This is not a problem for a discourse in which the judgments of competent judges are regarded merely as an input to critical discussion. Discourse can bring untoward influences out into the open – even those which agents are not aware of – and it can correct mistakes that are caused by them. It can also make use of the sensitivities and knowledge of people who are directly involved in relevant moral situations.

A competent judge, then, is someone who is intelligent enough and sensitive enough to the needs and feelings of others to make moral appraisals which others find intelligible and to understand the appraisals of others. She is reasonably well-informed about the situations she is judging and has appropriate background knowledge (though this information or knowledge need not be complete or error free). She is able and willing to reason and test her conclusions in the way that Rawls describes (though she will not necessarily do this without making errors), and able and willing to reflect critically on her assumptions and judgments in the light of her experiences and more general considerations. These are necessary conditions for participation in critical discourse, but not sufficient. We cannot suppose that the judgments and generalisations of competent judges, so defined, will necessarily count as ethical positions worth considering in critical discourse. For some of them may depend logically on doctrines which others cannot accept as rational bases for belief.

What should be said about views which are well-reasoned and sincerely motivated but depend on religious canons or other ideologies? It would be a mistake, I think, to assume that people who reason within the framework of a religious or some other kind of ideology cannot be competent judges, at least as so far defined. The religious judge need not be irrational or unbending; she may be prepared to question her ethical judgments; she may be prepared to argue with others, accept criticisms and learn from experience. But her conclusions and justifications rest ultimately upon her religious belief – on the authority of the Word of God or some such thing. These beliefs, after all, are central to her life and she naturally relies on them to guide her moral judgment and behaviour. The problem is that those who do not share her beliefs or do not regard reference to a sacred text as a relevant justification, will not feel obliged to regard the judgments which depend on these justifications as worthy of consideration. They might engage in critical conversation with her, but she is not really part of *their* discourse. Does this mean that there are many different critical discourses depending on framework of belief, or that her judgments are irrational or non-rational for reasons not yet discussed? However, if such individuals are to be ruled out as competent judges then there must be a good reason for doing so. We do not want to exclude positions from critical discourse just because they are unacceptable to the majority.

In his discussion of the requirements of judgment, Rawls insists, as we have seen, that a competent judge should not use her interests as a measure for judging the worth of the interests of others (Rawls 1951: 179). This could be understood merely to rule out views which favour, without adequate justification, particular individuals or groups. But Rawls could mean 'interest' to include not merely personal interests but ideals and ideologies. If so his requirement rules out positions which require for their justification a reference to a system of belief that others cannot be expected to accept. So understood the requirement would amount to insisting on what Nagel calls 'higher level impartiality' (Nagel 1987: 234).

Nagel claims that this requirement, at least in some contexts, is a rational one. A religious person may be entitled to live her life in accordance with her religious convictions and be satisfied with her religious justification for her actions. However, if she wants to persuade others that a moral position she holds is right, or reach an agreement with them about what moral principles should govern their behaviour towards each other, then she is going to have to find reasons for her moral views that they can accept as appropriate justifications. Since she knows that these others do not share her religion and that there are no rational means of persuading them to do so, she will be forced to transcend her religious framework of justification and either find reasons for her position which others can appreciate or adopt a position that is more likely to be acceptable.

Nagel is making a number of assumptions. One of them is that individuals are motivated to achieve higher level impartiality. This is not always so. An individual may be determined not to 'compromise' her religious beliefs by engaging in 'secular' justifications; she may even regard this as a sinful thing to do. If she refuses to transcend her framework, then I do not think that there are any rational means of persuading her to do so. Once again we run up against the problem that all attempts to characterise rationality are circular. However, those who insist on regarding the premises of their ethical positions as beyond question, will also not accept the rationality requirements of a procedure which insists that all beliefs are fallible and must be open to critical examination. Since they are not prepared to take seriously the criticisms of their assumptions, they are by choice not participants in critical discourse.

More important, Nagel is also assuming that achieving higher level impartiality is possible. I have argued that this assumption is problematic because it seems to require that an individual do what she cannot do: abstract from or overcome the influence of her situation. Situation is going to include religious belief and other ideals and ideologies. Moral judgment depends upon how people live their moral lives and respond to the cases they encounter, and for many people these responses can't be separated from their religious convictions or other ideals. So even if an individual is able and willing to give a non-religious justification for her point of view, her way of perceiving and appraising, responding to criticisms and drawing lessons from her life is going to be affected by her system of belief. A critic might argue that this means that *any* attempt to transcend situation and achieve impartiality, not just the monological one, is suspect. I will try to show that this is wrong.

A distinction should be made between views that are influenced by religion or other doctrines and those whose justification logically depends on reference to canons of belief. Imagine a person whose life has been profoundly affected by her religious beliefs. One of the most important moral ideas she regards herself as obtaining from her religion is a respect for human life. Her religion has given her the conviction that each life is precious and irreplaceable. Her way of regarding other people and responding to them is affected by her belief that their lives are sacred, and that they have a value which cannot be measured and should not be compromised. This conviction affects her treatment of many moral issues. She is horrified by those who regard their own lives or the lives of others as not having much value; she abhors policies which treat individuals as if they were the same or as replaceable units. She regards abortion and euthanasia as tragic, though not necessarily as always wrong.

This person's belief in the preciousness of life is clearly not a dogma. She does not hold it simply because her religion tells her to; nor does she treat it as a doctrine to be referred to like the articles of a catechism. She is prepared to accept all of the requirements of rationality imposed by Rawls and others. Moreover, this belief is integrated into her moral life; it guides her in her response to others, and she interprets and re-interprets its meaning and requirements as she deals with the problems she encounters. The sensitivity to others that it fosters, the insights that it makes possible, confirms her confidence in it. She thinks that it is the right view and that the judgments she makes from its perspective are sound, and for this reason thinks that others, including those who do not share her faith, should accept it. She will try to persuade them by showing them what difference the view could make to their lives and their judgments; she will argue for it by reference to reasons which she believes everyone should appreciate. The view that she presents to critical discourse is not *inferred* from her religious beliefs. For it can be supported by non-religious reasons and accepted by those who do not have her religious beliefs (or any religious beliefs). This does not mean that she has *transcended* her religious outlook. It continues to influence her moral perceptions and judgments.

The exclusion of views from discourse just because they are affected by religious and other ideologies would be difficult to justify. However, the influence of such ideals and doctrines on ethical views is clearly a major source of ethical disagreement. This acknowledgment provides sceptics with an opportunity to renew their attack on ethical rationality by arguing that the attempt of an individual to make her views acceptable to others is a fruitless exercise. Critical discourse, according to their view, cannot achieve impartial, objective judgments; it cannot even be a staging post on the way to such judgments. It is nothing more than an arena for displaying differences. If participants think that they are accomplishing something when they discuss and argue with each other, then this is simply a mistake – an illusion created by the view from the inside.

What the sceptical view ignores is the way in which religious and other beliefs can lead to moral insights – to positions which even those who think differently can appreciate as making a contribution to discourse. Let us suppose that the person described above loses her faith. Nevertheless, she will probably not abandon her belief in the preciousness of human life, or the ways of perceiving and judging associated with this belief. She is likely to regard the attitude towards human life that her religion gave her as extremely important; she thinks that it has enabled her to appreciate and value others properly and that her views about value have led her to make decisions and judgments which, on later reflection, seem right. She does not think that only a religious person could have the insights her religion gave her, but she realises that *she* might not have had them if she had not been religious.

What I am suggesting is that religious beliefs, ideals and ideologies, like other individual characteristics and experiences, can be the source of insights – not just for the individual who has them, but for other participants in discourse. This does not mean that others will agree with the moral views that arise from these insights. They have their own ways of perceiving, their own insights. But it does mean that the sceptic is wrong to suppose that individuals in discourse have nothing much to say to each other or that the objective of finding a point of view which somehow incorporates all the insights individuals contribute to discourse is mistaken.

Impartiality, according to the ethical collectivist, is not going to be achieved simply by discussion and criticism. Nevertheless, as a criterion for determining what judgments critical discourse must consider (and which it need not consider), Nagel's requirement seems right: a moral position is considerable, as far as critical discourse is concerned, only if it can be given a justification without reference to doctrines or ideals which are not themselves rationally defensible. A considerable position is not a dogma; it can be argued for in the framework of a method like that of Rawls or Daniels. This doesn't necessarily mean that it is cogent. Participants in critical discourse may discover that it is not well-supported by evidence, that it is biased or ill informed. On the other hand, judgments about which positions are rationally defensible, and therefore considerable, do not require that participants reach a consensus about ideals or ideologies.

The right and the good

The acceptance of Nagel's requirement (as interpreted) means that ethical collectivism, like many theories about morality, has to make a distinction between the 'right' and the 'good': between questions about right and wrong and questions about the nature of a good life, and has to insist that it is the primary job of moral reasoning to determine what is right – to determine how individuals with different ideals and ideologies should behave towards each other. This means that it is questions of right which are the subject matter of discourse, and not attempts to answer questions about how to live a good life or what ideals an individual should adopt. This familiar view about the subject of ethical reasoning is a common one. It is held by philosophers who are as divided in their views about ethics as are Hare and Habermas.[2] Nevertheless, the distinction gives rise to problems – especially for ethical collectivists.

People disagree about what is good, but they also disagree about what is right. The idea that people with different ideals can nevertheless reach agreement about how they should treat each other is a vain hope, at least for monological ethics, and leads to doubts about the usefulness of the distinction. Ethical collectivism does not suppose that individuals can reach a distributive agreement about what is right, but it does treat the disagreements differently. Views about what is right are the subject matter of discourse; views about the good are not. Participants in constructive discourse are expected to reach a collective agreement about what is right, but not about what is good. A natural question to ask is what justifies this difference of treatment? Why should it be our ideas of the right and not our ideas of the good that are reconciled through discourse? A justification of difference in treatment must be a reason for thinking that judgments about the good really are different from judgments about right – one that doesn't depend on the supposition that we can reach a distributive agreement about right but not about the good.

One idea about how to make the distinction is to point out that we think that ideas about right should be universalisable, but we don't think this about ideas of the good. My good is truly my own, and I would not expect others, who have different characteristics and predilections, to adopt it. They will have ideas of their own about what is a good life. The problem with this way of making the distinction is that ideas of the right are also affected by personal characteristics and ideals. The religious person, as we have seen, is likely to be influenced by her religious ideals when she makes moral judgments or acts as a moral agent. Why then should we suppose that 'what is right?' demands an answer that everyone should accept while 'what is good?' does not?

Ideas of the good, it might be argued, are personal in a deeper, incorrigible way. Suppose you know a businessman who dedicated himself to making as much money as possible and is consequently ruining his health and his relations with others. You might try to persuade him that he would be better off if he had other ends: that he would be happier and more fulfilled. But if, after carefully considering your opinions, he decides that getting rich, doing down his rivals, means more to him than anything else, then what more can you say? There are limits, it seems, to how much individuals can achieve by arguing that someone's choice of a good is mistaken. This means that basic ends can't be fully justified by reasons, and it is this feature of ideas of the good which makes them inappropriate candidates for universalisation and an unsuitable topic for a moral discourse which aims at rationally justified belief.

The idea that a person's fundamental conception of the good is non-rational has sometimes been challenged. Some philosophers do believe that if an individual properly considers all of the likely consequences of having a particular good, and in addition reflects on how his or her life would go if she adopted other ends, if she had full information about what each particular idea of the good entails for herself and others, then she would be in a position to make a fully rational choice about ends.[3] Perhaps the problem with the businessman is that he has not adequately reflected on his choice. Perhaps he has not paraded before his mind in a complete or vivid way the consequences of life as he is living it. (Has he really considered what his life will be like when he becomes old or if he loses his money?) Perhaps he has not thought seriously of other alternatives or attempted to picture to himself what his life would be like if he adopted them. If he did all this, it might be claimed, then he would agree that his present ends are unsatisfactory and it would be rational for him to come to this conclusion. If ends can be rationally chosen, this would not entail that they are not personal. It could be rational for individuals to choose different ends depending on character and predilections. However, the distinction between the right and the good would become much more difficult to maintain, and the restriction of discourse to questions of right more difficult to defend.

The view that the choice of fundamental ends can be completely rational is mistaken. The reason has to do with the role ideas of the good play in an individual's life. What a person thinks is fundamentally good will influence how she lives her life, the characteristics she cultivates, and thus what identity she develops. Ideas of the good are implicated in our development as individuals – they help to determine our tastes, our attitudes and our interpretations of the world. This means that a person cannot, without circularity, justify her fundamental values by reference to her tastes, inclinations or characteristics, by what she thinks is worth emulating, or what creed she is inclined to follow. For her idea of the good is partially responsible for her tastes, inclinations and interpretations. If a person is actually questioning her direction in life and trying to decide what she should value, then the under-determination of ideas of the good by rational considerations becomes obvious. For she knows that she is not constrained in her choice by her existing characteristics and predilections. She may choose to try to make herself into a different kind of person. She might even choose to strive towards an ideal she knows she can never achieve, or even one that no human being could achieve (like a life of extreme saintliness). We may dislike her choice, or think that it has immoral or other undesirable consequences. If the businessman wants to become a competent ethical agent, then he has good reason to be critical of some of his ideals and attitudes – those which encourage him to be insensitive to the needs and interests of others. But considered simply as an individual choice, a particular idea of the good cannot be dismissed as irrational.

What this means is that fundamental values are best understood as commitments. They are decisions about how to live a life and what desires and characteristics to cultivate, and by their nature they cannot be fully rational.[4] This is different from saying that these choices are unmotivated. An individual may be drawn to an ideal or a way of life; she may feel that her idea of the good suits her. But when it comes to justification, she will have to acknowledge that her commitment lacks a fully rational explanation. This does not mean that no reasoning is possible concerning choice of fundamental values. We can and do criticise views about the good. Values can be based upon false beliefs about the world (like, for example, the ideal of promoting racial purity), and individuals can have misconceptions about what their ideals entail. When they discover their mistakes they will, as rational agents, want to make revisions to their conception of what is valuable. However, sooner or later reasoning about values has to come to an end, and we are forced to accept that others make their own decisions about how to live. This is why the businessman can, without being irrational, resist our ideas about how he should live his life.

Methods for deciding what values to hold are also under-determined by reasons. We would doubt the seriousness of someone who determines her values by consulting a horoscope or by flipping a coin. (Pascal's wager is regarded by some people as providing an inappropriate motivation for religious belief simply because it is a wager.) We find it difficult to believe that a person can make a real commitment in this way; commitments, we think, must come from the heart. But this is merely a psychological generalisation. If a person who makes a decision about her good in a non-standard way demonstrates that she is really prepared to live by it, then it is a mistake to complain about the way she made it. The same can be said about the commitments of communities. From a political point of view, it seems desirable that groups make decisions about their ends by democratic means, for then everyone will feel that their views count, and will be better prepared to accept the duties entailed by the decision. However, if members of a group all feel that it is right and proper to determine their objectives by other means – by consulting an oracle or accepting the decision of a charismatic leader – then whatever else we might say about their decision-making method, we cannot say that it is irrational.

If the choice of basic ends is a commitment, then the common assumption that ideas of the good are deeply personal is confirmed. And so is the distinction between questions about right – morality proper – and questions about the good life. The answers individuals give to questions about what is right are supposed to have a wholly rational justification, but the answers they give to basic questions about the good cannot be wholly justified. Nevertheless, once we abandon the idea that individuals can and should transcend their idea of the good when making moral judgments, we are able to acknowledge that there is an intimate relation between an individual's good and her views about right. Her ability to make moral judgments and justify them depends upon her perspective, and this is bound to be affected by her ideas of the good, or at least by the characteristics and predilection that she has developed because of her ideas of the good. Basic values are part of a person's situation; they shape the point of view from which an ethical stance is taken.[5]

The intimate relation between right and good might be regarded as a reason for re-opening the debate about the rationality of moral judgment. If moral judgment depends upon commitments which are themselves non-rational, then does this mean that it is also non-rational? After all, the reason for thinking that judgments about tastes (in the example on p. 59) are not wholly rational is that the sensations themselves are merely consequences of genetic or developmental quirks. If ideas of the good are equally arbitrary, then surely the moral judgments arising from them must for the same reason fail to be wholly rational. The sceptic might make the same point in another way. If moral judgments depend on ideas of the good and these cannot be rationally justified, then surely Harman is right to think that our moral judgments are relative to our ideologies, and therefore cannot be rational in the way that empirical beliefs can be rational.

These sceptical objections are based upon two confusions. They confuse ideology as a premise of ethical reasoning with ideology as an influence on our ethical perceptions, and they confuse the reasons a person has for accepting an ideal with the reasons she has for thinking that her way of perceiving leads to moral insights. If an individual's ethical beliefs are logically deduced from an ideology which itself is placed beyond question, then the status of her moral judgments is indeed what Harman says it is: once we have determined that her judgments depend upon a fixed idea for which no acceptable justification can be given, there is no epistemological point to further discussion. She believes what she believes, and that's the end of it. She is in the same position as the religious person who justifies her moral judgments by reference to religious texts. We cannot refute her judgments, but on the other hand, we do not have to take them seriously. The very fact that her beliefs rest on non-rational premises rules her out of critical discourse. On the other hand, a person can be influenced in her ethical judging by her idea of the good – in the sense that it affects what she thinks important, the way she lives her life and develops her personality – and yet not depend for the justification of her beliefs on any ideological assumption. She can provide justifications which other rational agents, though they have different ideas of the good, are compelled to take seriously.

The second distinction, between the reasons (or lack of reasons) for making a particular value commitment and the reasons that we have for thinking that a value commitment contributes to insightful ethical judgment, is equally important. A person's situation can be arbitrary in the sense that it depends upon factors beyond her control (like where she was born) or on value commitments which cannot be fully justified. And yet, we can have good reason to think that being in this situation enables her to make insightful judgments which others ought to take into account. The difference between judgments of taste, however sophisticated, and moral judgments is that I do not have to think that the reliability of my taste perceptions (once they have been developed and refined) are called into question by the fact that others taste things differently, but the reasons we have for thinking that the moral judgments of others are insightful are also reasons for not being entirely satisfied with our own.

Some value commitments are more likely to be conducive to good ethical judgment than others. The businessman who commits himself wholly to becoming rich is likely to be underdeveloped as far as his moral sensibilities are concerned. A person who regards the care of others as the most important goal of her life is likely to have developed to a high degree the ability to recognise certain kinds of need. The ways in which individuals develop their personality according to their ideas of the good may make them better ethical judges in some cases than in others. The businessman, though bad at understanding the feelings of others, may have a highly developed appreciation of the nuances of contract and promise-making. Not all situations or value commitments are conducive to good ethical judgment (something that critical discourse will make clear), and it seems reasonable to believe that there are some values which all those who aim to be good ethical judges should adopt: such as the ability to engage in critical self-reflection and sensitivity to the needs of others.[6] However, it seems reasonable to believe that insightful ethical judgments can come from individuals who are influenced in their thinking and living by many different value commitments.

Since there is an epistemological justification for treating questions about right differently from those about good, ethical collectivists can with good conscience make use of Nagel's requirement as a necessary condition for a position being something which critical discourse should consider. The only ethical positions worthy of being considered in critical discourse are those which can be given a justification which is logically independent of the ideals or doctrines which influence the life and thought of those who put forward the positions. The requirement rules out positions whose justification logically depends on a reference to a creed or an idea of the good. It does not rule out positions which are influenced by an ideal in the sense that *having* that position depends psychologically on a perspective which is formed, or partly formed, by this ideal.

Are there any other necessary conditions for a position being considered in discourse to add to those already discussed? Some people will insist that the restrictions so far imposed are not yet sufficient to ensure that participants in discourse will be able to gain anything substantial from criticism or discussion, let alone reach an agreement (distributive or collective). What is needed, they might argue, is a *moral* limitation on what positions can be considered. For even a collective agreement, at least of the kind that ethical collectivists are aiming for, will be impossible for individuals whose moral opinions are *very* different from each other.

Rawls' requirement that competent judges treat the interests of others as equal to their own (and thus equal to each other) could be understood as a substantial moral premise: that individuals deserve equal consideration. If we adopt this moral assumption then this means that no position will be considered in critical discourse if it is incompatible with the assumption that individuals are of equal moral worth. The question is whether it is necessary or desirable to insist that all participants in discourse accept this moral idea or any other moral premise.

Whether moral assumptions are necessary depends upon whether discourse could have an acceptable outcome without them. It may be the case that individuals will not be able to reach a conclusion that all can endorse (even a constructed conclusion) without a common moral starting point. They will find that any proposed conclusion to discourse will be completely unacceptable to some participants. This would mean that there are not going to be universal moral principles which every rational person has to accept – even among people who agree about requirements of rationality. Ethical collectivism cannot rule out the possibility that moral principles acceptable to people in one culture or society will not be acceptable to those in another. But we should not be too quick to assume that cultural relativism is right. In fact, ethical collectivists have reason to resist this assumption. The idea that individuals ought to be respected as equals has been the subject of debate, and even among those who now take it for granted, the meaning and implications of this moral position are still a matter of contention. To treat a matter of moral controversy as a requirement of ethical rationality not only assumes that the issue is settled and nothing has to be said to those who disagree. It also represents an ethical matter as a meta-ethical assumption; it commits a kind of logical impropriety.

So it is better for ethical collectivists to begin with the 'universalist' supposition that ethical relativism is false and that participants in discourse will be able to arrive at principles which apply to and must be applied by everyone. (What might make them abandon this position I will consider in Chapter 5.) They are in a far better position to defend universalism than are those who take a monological approach to ethical knowledge. Let us assume, then, that the conditions so far discussed – Rawls' requirements for competent judges (modified in the ways suggested) and Nagel's restriction on positions and justifications – are jointly sufficient for determining what positions should be considered in critical discourse.

Critical discourse

The inputs to critical discourse are the considerable positions reached by competent judges on a set of related issues. They are positions which satisfy the requirements imposed upon individual judgment. Participants in critical discourse examine these products of individual reasoning and the justifications for them; they argue, bring to bear relevant background theories and information, criticise and amend them. Some positions brought to discourse will be eliminated by criticisms, others will be amended, and some new ones may be advanced. The output of critical discourse is the 'cogent' positions which survive critical discussion and from which a conclusion will finally be constructed.

Critical discourse serves two functions. First of all, it puts individual judgments to the test and thus ensures that they are as good as they can be (or as good as critical discussion can presently make them). As a test for moral judgments it is a necessary part of any decision-procedure, at least for non-ideal judges. Rawls assumes that competent judges will criticise and discuss each other's judgments and conclusions, though he doesn't have much to say about the role or nature of dialogue. Advocates of wide reflective equilibrium similarly assume that individuals will criticise each other's conclusions in the light of theories and observations at all levels of justification. For Habermas discourse ensures that each individual is forced to confront criticism and justify the presuppositions of her communicative actions whenever they are questioned. However, for ethical collectivists critical discourse also serves a second function: it is supposed to arrive at a complete set of cogent positions from which an agreed conclusion can be constructed. This is why it has to be regarded as a distinct stage of the ethical collectivist procedure and not merely a taken-for-granted background to individual decision-making. The second function of critical discourse will not only affect the way in which participants understand what they are doing, but it will also influence the process itself: what participants have to consider and what they are supposed to agree on (and what they are not expected to agree about).

The role critical discourse plays within an ethical collectivist procedure means that participants will have different aims from those of participants in more familiar discourses. First of all, in critical discourse participants discuss moral *generalisations* – the conclusions of their own reasoning and reflection on a range of moral problems. Their ultimate objective is to discover principles or guidelines which will guide their future actions and judgments. Critical examination of moral positions will sometimes require participants to reconsider how individual cases have been or could be judged. But making judgments about individual cases or discussing them is not the central concern of critical discourse. Second, critical discourse is supposed to examine and debate *moral* positions. It is not a dialogue in which individuals represent or advance their particular interests. Rawls thinks that a competent judge ought to inquire into the needs and interests of those whose case she is judging, and this is likely to require that she holds a conversation with them. Others think that more extensive and continuous discussions about attitudes and states of mind are necessary. Intercourse of this kind is not critical discourse. It is part of the process that individuals go through in order to establish their own position. Their minds are made up, at least provisionally, when they present their views in critical discourse. Participants may discuss why a judge interpreted interests in the way she did and may question whether she assessed the interests of those whose case she judged in the correct way. But it is not the central purpose of discourse to identify or interpret the needs, wants or aims of individuals.

The individuals who participate in critical discourse are assumed to be 'competent' as this is understood in the previous section. They have to be able to make moral assessments and justify them, argue in a more or less rational way and follow rational arguments. They have to be willing and able to produce reasons for their position which others can recognise as good reasons. On the other hand, individuals do not have to be terribly good at argument in order to participate in discourse. Participants are not competing with each other to get their position endorsed by the general will. They know that this is not likely to happen. The primary purpose of discourse is to discover the cogent views about a particular range of moral issues. So the objective of the participants is not only to argue for the cogency of their own view but to understand the positions of others and determine whether these other views are cogent. This will sometimes involve searching for possible justifications and arguments for positions which are not so well-defended by those who put them forward. Critical discourse is much more of a co-operative enterprise than ethical discourse as it is usually conducted or conceived.

The fact that critical discourse is co-operative helps to meet a difficulty for discourse theories stressed by Young (1995: 136ff.). She thinks that discourse ethics, as it is usually conceived, is bound to favour those who are articulate and accustomed to argument, and marginalise those who are not, and she advocates forms of communication which allow the less well-educated or articulate to express their points of view. The problem is that if the point of discourse is to arrive at justified beliefs – and not merely to express points of view – then there is no substitute for articulated positions, the giving of reasons and critical discussion. Critical discourse, because of its epistemological objective, cannot satisfy Young's desire that anyone be able to participate in discourse and represent their own point of view. It will not include everyone who happens to have an ethical opinion. For some opinions are not considerable ethical positions. And it allows individuals to present and argue for the positions of others – something that will be necessary if those who are inarticulate or bad at argument are to have their considerable views properly discussed.

Nevertheless, critical discourse does provide an answer to the problem which motivates Young's insistence on universal participation: the need to ensure that those who are oppressed or marginalised have a voice. If constructive discourse is to reach a satisfactory result then it must have supplied to it all positions worthy of consideration (or at least all that participants can assemble at a particular time and place). Participants must, at least, have reason to believe that all cogent views will be discovered and articulated by critical discourse, and this means that they cannot be satisfied with a discourse in which only the dominant views are presented or only the views of a particular group. They will have to ensure that people from marginalised groups, people who are likely to have minority ethical views, are also participants and that their positions are regarded with respect (though not uncritically). The willingness of participants in discourse to listen to other voices is not motivated by charity or curiosity. That they do so is an epistemological necessity.

Those whose positions must be included are not only the oppressed and the marginalised, but individuals who suffer from a worse disability. Participants must also ensure that they present and discuss views of people who are no longer alive. Ethical conversation is, after all, an ongoing process to which past generations have contributed and participants will sometimes find it necessary or worthwhile to represent ideas and considerable views that come from the past even if no one now advocates them.

However, the requirement of 'completeness' – the need for critical discourse to evaluate all relevant considerable points of view and therefore arrive at a complete set of cogent positions concerning a related set of issues – raises some obvious theoretical and practical difficulties. The monological approach presupposes that competent individuals can take their well-motivated ethical beliefs for granted until they encounter someone who disagrees with them. At this point they are expected to engage in dialogue, answer criticisms, and amend or give up their beliefs if necessary. Discourse is an occasional episode in a person's ethical life, and Habermas and others who advocate discourse ethics do not require that we hold a kind of universal public meeting in order to decide ethical matters. Discourse ethics, as they conceive it, doesn't involve crowd scenes. On the other hand, ethical collectivism, by denying that individuals are justified in believing what seems to them to be true, requires that individuals actually participate together in critical discourse. For how else can they collect all cogent views on a related set of issues and know that they have done so? But if this means that *everyone* has to participate then the procedures advocated by ethical collectivism seem obviously impractical, if not totally bizarre (especially if 'everyone' includes the dead).

Furthermore, it will be objected that not everyone can present a view to discourse. For one thing, not everyone has the capabilities of a competent judge. Also excluded will be those who are not capable of putting forward *any* point of view: foetuses, babies, small children, the severely mentally disabled, future generations, animals, the environment and other beings affected by our actions. How, then, can discourse achieve, or even aspire to, completeness?

This objection is based upon a misunderstanding of the purpose of critical discourse. It is not a dialogue in which individuals represent their own interests. It is not a democratic procedure which requires that everyone expresses his or her opinion or casts a vote. Not everyone has to participate in discourse because not everyone has a distinct moral position to present (though some may have more than one). Furthermore, individuals can represent others; they can present the moral positions of others to discourse, and they can argue for moral positions which take into account beings who cannot speak for themselves. The question of how these beings should be treated is going to be central to some discourses. And the conclusions that participants in constructive discourse finally reach (given that all relevant cogent views are taken into account and the discourse is properly conducted) will be what individuals are justified in believing are true. The fact that we cannot carry on dialogues with animals, future generations, etc. may sometimes mean that we will be uncertain about their needs and interests, and this may affect our confidence in the moral conclusions we reach. But this is an uncertainty that the proponents of any ethical theory have to live with.

What participants in critical discourse have to ensure is that they have considered all relevant positions about the range of issues in question. They will never be absolutely certain that they have done so. Views can be wrongly excluded because of prejudice, social pressure, or because no one is now capable of appreciating them. Participants may not be sure where to look in order to find views that should be represented. Those who represent the views of others may not do so adequately. These are problems which beset any enterprise aiming for truth. They do not undermine confidence in our ability to make progress towards that goal so long as there are practical steps that can be taken to detect errors, better appreciate the positions of others, and find and include positions which have been ignored. These methods for improving performance and making progress towards completeness should be capable of development and refinement as participants gain experience in resolving ethical disputes through discourse.

Where we look for distinct moral perspectives is a matter of common sense and experience. Experience of moral conflict suggests that people who have different social positions and backgrounds, a different education and upbringing, are likely to have different moral perspectives on many issues. Differences in gender, class, social role, religious or ethnic background seem to be highly correlated with differences in moral opinion, though some of these differences could turn out to be the result of misinformation or error. It will be a good idea, as a first approximation, to ensure that discourse includes people who have different backgrounds in respects that seem relevant (or at least that their views are represented). Any practical attempt to hold a critical discourse that satisfies ethical collectivist requirements will require a continual effort to discover and include other points of view. This requirement is not motivated by a well-meaning liberal desire to allow people in minority groups to have their say or to ensure that everyone is represented in a political process. It is driven by epistemological considerations: the recognition that arriving at justified ethical beliefs must be a collective endeavour, and that nothing relevant to achieving this end should be excluded.

There can be no guaranteed end to the process of including and criticising ethical views, and thus no discourse to end all discourse. This means that no ethical conclusion can be regarded as final and unchallengeable – but this is another uncertainty that all conscientious agents have to learn to live with. Like most other ethical and empirical theories of knowledge, ethical collectivism is fallibalist. It claims that there is no theory about what is right and wrong, however well we can now justify it, which is so certain and beyond question, that it is inconceivable that it ever be revised. To be a fallibalist does not mean that we have to doubt everything that can be doubted, thus suspending belief in our ethical or empirical judgments indefinitely. We are entitled to live by the beliefs we can now justify. Nor do we have to suppose that all the judgments that we regard as basic are likely some day to be overthrown. It is just as unlikely to suppose that ethical discourse will some day reach the conclusion that torturing a child is not wrong as it is to suppose that some day empirical research will discover that snow is not white. What will be debated in discourse is how such beliefs should be explained and interpreted, and how they are related to other judgments and generalisations.

Learning how to appreciate the views of others is something that all of us try to do and sometimes we have reason to believe that we have succeeded. Nevertheless, if critical discourse is to prepare the way for constructive discourse, then participants have to be able to reach agreement about what views are cogent. This agreement, like the one about requirements of rationality, must be a distributive one. For if an individual does not think that a position is cogent, she will not believe that it should be considered in constructive discourse and thus will not regard the conclusion reached by constructive discourse as correct. And if she thinks that there are cogent views which have not been included then she will also reasonably reject the results of constructive discourse.

A sceptic might object that the likelihood of individuals agreeing on what views are cogent is just about as small as the likelihood that they will agree in their moral judgments. But this does not seem to be true. To judge that a view is cogent it is not necessary for participants in discourse to agree with it or even think that it is very much like their own. They have to be able to judge that the reasons given for the view are good reasons – that they adequately support the view – and that objections and criticisms can plausibly be answered by those who hold it. They have to determine, in other words, that the view is not the result of prejudice or bad argument, that its advocates have taken relevant information into account and are able to give reasonable answers to arguments against it. We know that those who participate in debates and discussions are frequently able to recognise their opponents' reasoning as good reasoning even when they disagree with their conclusions. But to counter the sceptical objection we have to consider why participants might not agree in their judgments about cogency, and what, if anything, can be done about it.

One reason why participants may not agree is because they do not, or cannot, understand some of the positions or the justifications given for them. I have argued (in Chapter 3) that there is no reason to think that individuals *cannot* learn to understand the positions of others, especially if they engage in discourse with these others. Nevertheless, there could be views *so* different from our own that we will never be able to appreciate them, however hard we try. We might not be able to understand why a particular position should be regarded as a moral point of view, or we may think that the views of some others, or their reasons, are irrelevant or wrong-headed, and no matter how much we communicate we fail to find a common basis for understanding. Some people argue that this is likely to happen between people from different cultures. I have allowed that cultural relativism could turn out to be true, and persistent failure of communication is one reason which might persuade us to be relativists. On the other hand, we shouldn't assume too quickly that communication is impossible. In discourse gaps of understanding can often be filled by well-motivated people.

However, even if well-motivated individuals can appreciate each other's positions, they may in fact fail to do so. For participants in discourse are less than ideal agents whose imagination and experience are limited and who may not be used to communicating with others who are very different from themselves. However, this familiar individual limitation will not necessarily prevent participants from agreeing about what views are cogent. For if individuals are rational they will acknowledge that their understanding is limited, and will find it reasonable in some cases to trust the judgment of others. Let us say that x and y, both competent agents, are able to reach agreement in many cases about which views are cogent. But x thinks that z's view, a view that y is unable to understand, should also be regarded as cogent, and y knows that x, because of his background or experiences is in a better position to understand z's views than she is. It is reasonable for her to trust x's judgment and to agree that z's view may be cogent. If others whom she also trusts to get things right agree with x's judgment, then her belief that z's view is cogent is further confirmed. She will, to be sure, be unsatisfied with this situation; she will want to understand z, and may eventually be able to do so – either through further discussion or by having experiences which provide her with insights into z's way of thinking. But meanwhile she has reason to think it rational to accept the judgment of x and others whom she has reason to trust.

This indirect way of making judgments about cogency depends upon the existence of individuals like x who are able and willing to appreciate what is beyond the comprehension of others. Such people may not exist, or may not be heeded. Some individuals or groups may not have their views treated seriously simply because no one is prepared to make the effort to do so. Participants in discourse can fail to reach agreement about cogency because of pre-conceived ideas about what kinds of views are worth considering, a hostility or lack of sympathy for those who are unconventional, or an inability to appreciate those whose experiences are very different from their own. Those who are sceptical about getting an agreed result concerning cogency from critical discourse may be worried, not about whether appreciation is theoretically possible, but whether participants, being what they are, are likely to achieve it. The problem, they might argue, is not simply that even the most competent agents have their failings but that the social situation of participants in a discussion is likely to weigh the scales in favour of mainstream views, the views of the powerful, the well-educated and articulate. These people will dominate critical and constructive discourse, and the views of socially marginal people will be dismissed or denigrated. At its worst, sceptics might argue, critical discourse will simply confirm the racist or sexist views of the mainstream. Even at its best it will tend to treat some views with more consideration than others. If so, leaving it up to participants in discourse to decide what ethical views deserve to be taken seriously is a dangerous and epistemologically unsatisfactory way to proceed. It may be better to rely on individual judgment about what is plausible.

Further reasons for this sceptical conclusion come from studies of group psychology (Janis 1982). Discourse involves a relationship between individuals, and the reasoning of people who interact with each other is invariably affected by social or personal factors. Individuals with high status or power frequently have an influence on the judgment of others out of proportion to the cogency of their views. Individuals can also be affected in their judgments by irrelevant features of persons (effects which may also have to do with class or status): by the way others present their views, by their personal appearance, manner, congeniality, etc. Individuals generally want others to approve of them, particularly those others whom they regard as important or sympathetic. They are predisposed to appreciate the views of those they find attractive, charismatic or sympathetic. They will not be so ready to appreciate the views of those they find unsympathetic, unattractive or alien. The problem is not just that these influences exist, but that they are not generally recognised or acknowledged by those concerned. Power and other kinds of influence can be exercised unconsciously or in subtle and indirect ways, and individuals are not generally aware of how their reasoning or their views about what is reasonable are affected. Because individuals want to be regarded as rational and autonomous they have a motive for not acknowledging the influences that act on them. They will resist any suggestion that their conclusions are anything else but rational, and are thus unlikely to discover that they are not. So discourse, according to the sceptic, is unlikely to achieve a rational agreement about anything.

What really follows from these psychological considerations? Not that discourse is *especially* untrustworthy. The problem of prejudice and the distortions caused by social relations are not peculiar to a discourse ethics. Any community of inquiry, whether scientific or ethical, is subject to the same irrationalities, and the individual alone in her study can be as deeply affected by group perversions as participants in a dialogue. What is essential for rational inquiry is that there be techniques available for detecting error and prejudice, and methods for overcoming untoward influences, or at least making progress towards this objective. A decision-procedure for non-ideal agents cannot expect to eliminate all errors and produce conclusions that are beyond the reach of doubt, but it must at least show how judgments can be tested and improved so that those who use the method are justified in thinking that their results are rational until they discover good reasons for doubt.

To deal with hidden irrationalities and subtle influences, critical discourse (and any kind of inquiry) needs not only methods for detecting error, but ways of developing methods to detect and correct error. To start with we have familiar means of detecting and dealing with fallacies in argument and for recognising the more obvious forms of prejudice. We also have at hand ways of recognising when someone is exercising untoward influence on a discourse and ways of preventing the suppression of views (e.g. by maintaining anonymity of participants). From this starting point we can develop more sophisticated techniques for identifying and overcoming irrationality. Brandt's cognitive psychotherapy (interpreted in a commonsense way) is one method for recognising our own irrationalities, and it is reasonable to suppose that we can develop more sophisticated tests for revealing insensitivities, conceptual blindness or rigidity of thought. Scientific studies of group behaviour have uncovered some of the subtle influences of social relations on the way people present their views and attend to each other in discourse. And once these distortions are discovered we can investigate methods for overcoming them. (One suggestion might be preventing participants from directly encountering each other.) There is no reason to think that we cannot make progress towards rationality in individual thought and discourse, even though we know that our conclusions will probably never be entirely free of bias.

We can reasonably assume that well-motivated participants in critical discourse can reach a justified agreement about what moral positions are cogent. So let us suppose that they have collected a set of positions which they have agreed are cogent – a set which is as complete as they can make it at this time and place. These positions are the input to another procedure which I call constructive discourse. How participants in constructive discourse are supposed to arrive at a conclusion that all can and must endorse as right is the subject of Chapter 5.

5

REQUIREMENTS OF ETHICAL REASONING: CONSTRUCTIVE DISCOURSE

Constructive discourse takes as input the ethical positions which have survived critical examination in critical discourse and from them it constructs a conclusion. The cogent positions taken or represented by participants in constructive discourse (and the justifications they give for them) can be regarded as data, and the position they construct the best explanation of these data.[1] In arriving at this best explanation participants must presume (unless they have good reasons for thinking otherwise) that each position is equally cogent and must be given an equal weight in the process of construction. For each has been subject to criticism and amendment in critical discourse and thus each counts as a partial but insightful ethical view. The conclusion reached by constructive discourse takes into account and accommodates all of these cogent views, but is not necessarily identical with any one of them.

Requirements of constructive discourse

In constructive discourse participants are searching for an agreed solution to a related set of moral problems, and this requires that they transcend their particular perspectives. The agreement they achieve will not come about because each person from his own perspective judges that a particular proposal is right. If a distributive agreement were possible then it would have been reached in critical discourse. There is good reason to believe that such a monological agreement is often *not* achievable. An impartial, objective position, if such a thing is possible, must be a collective accomplishment, something constructed from the positions of participants. Nevertheless, if the conclusion is well-constructed, if the conditions of constructive discourse are satisfied, then participants are entitled to regard it as true. They accept it as such not because they have changed their way of perceiving and now think, judging from their own intuitions and reflections, that the collective conclusion is correct. Individuals from their own standpoint may still have the *impression* that their own point of view is right. Transcendence of situation is not something that we can expect an individual to achieve.

95

Constructive discourse, and the epistemological considerations which motivate it, give them reason to think that their view from the inside is incorrect and that they should instead accept the conclusion of discourse as the right judgment about the moral matters in question.

The participants, we can assume, are the same or similar competent judges as those who participate in critical discourse. In general, we can assume that they represent their own ethical position(s), but there is no reason why they can't also represent the positions of others. I will also assume that they are capable of understanding the positions of others – at least sufficiently to enter into dialogue – and that they are motivated to reach a constructed conclusion. We do not have to assume that each individual fully appreciates the views of every other individual. Since discourse is a collective enterprise it is not necessary that each individual exercises exactly the same degree of competence. But it is important that everyone is understood by someone. For otherwise there will be no way of confirming or criticising the judgments that individuals have to make in discourse.

In constructive discourse participants are faced with a range of non-equivalent positions, some of which contradict each other, and different and sometimes opposing ideas about what is morally important and how the moral facts should be described. Since participants know that these views are partial, they have no reason to suppose that the right conclusion is identical with any one of them. So they will attempt to reach agreement by making proposals which take into account and accommodate aspects of each of the positions represented in discourse. These proposals can be thought of as hypotheses for explaining the data. We will assume that each participant is able and willing to put forward and justify such proposals, and that each can assess the proposals of others in relation to his or her own position, to judge how well it accommodates his particular concerns and whether it does this better or worse than other proposals. We are also assuming that these judgments of individuals can be assessed and criticised by others.

Each individual accepts that all positions offered to discourse are on an equal footing. Participants will naturally be concerned to ensure that their position is adequately considered (since this is the position that they are representing). But they are not competing with each other to skew the results in their favour. They have epistemological reasons for ensuring that the positions and proposals of others receive their due weight. Constructive discourse is a means by which individuals can move towards an agreed conclusion, proceeding from their own points of view. Each will propose a hypothesis which seems to him closer to the position of the other participants than is his own view, but at the same time is closer to his own position (given what he thinks is morally important) than are the positions represented by the others. The other agents will judge this hypothesis in the light of how well it meets the moral concerns which *their* views embody. Very likely they will not all be satisfied that the proposal does adequately deal with all of their concerns. So they in turn will put forward hypotheses which are better from their point of view than is his proposal.

We will assume that each participant can rank these proposals according to how close or distant they are to his own point of view and can present reasons for his ranking. Each also knows how others rank proposals and the reasons for their rankings. So each is in the position to aim at a proposal, or an amendment to a proposal, which can be ranked higher by those who ranked previous proposals low, and which is not regarded as being much worse than previous proposals by those who ranked these previous proposals highly. If all goes well constructive discourse will in this way approach a hypothesis which no one can improve on, judged from his point of view, without making it worse for some other(s) to a degree greater for these individuals (when judged from their own points of view) than the improvement is for him.

Reaching a conclusion by construction may seem like a complicated and dubious enterprise to those used to monological methods. However, it is not substantially different from the way in which an individual accommodates his disparate points of view when he is in more than one mind about how to resolve an ethical problem. A constructed conclusion is a kind of reflective equilibrium, and in some respects the process of arriving at it is similar to the method recommended by Rawls and Daniels. We can call the conclusion that constructive discourse aims to construct a 'dialogic equilibrium'. We have, on one hand, the positions which arise from different perspectives and, on the other, the proposals made in constructive discourse (or by an individual who wants to accommodate his different points of view). We aim to choose a proposal which best takes into account the represented positions, but do not regard any of these positions, or the proposals which attempt to accommodate them, as unquestionable truths (however much an individual wants to believe that a particular position or proposal is true). What we are looking for is a point of equilibrium, a proposal which treats each of the points of view with equal respect, but isn't (necessarily or generally) identical with any of them. The difference between reaching a reflective equilibrium, as this is usually understood, and reaching a constructed conclusion is that the former deals only with a more or less compatible set of moral intuitions (and background beliefs). Its task is to determine what generalisation best fits these intuitions, or most of them, when they are suitably re-interpreted and reassessed. Constructive discourse, whether it takes place in the mind of the individual or is conducted by a collective, has to deal with incompatible ethical positions which have already met the test of critical discourse. This means, firstly, that what has to be accommodated are not just intuitions but different and often incompatible positions, and secondly that we cannot treat them as we might treat our intuitions; we cannot simply ignore them or dismiss them when they don't fit into the framework we are motivated to adopt.

Reaching a dialogic equilibrium

The differences of opinion which an individual has with himself are not likely to be extensive or all that difficult to reconcile. Disagreements among individuals are going to be much more radical. A critic might well wonder how we can expect to reach a dialogic equilibrium among positions which are contradictory or drastically different. How, for example, can we expect to accommodate both those who think that abortion is seriously wrong and those who don't regard it as any kind of moral evil, or those who approve of capital punishment and those who think it is wrong? The very idea of accommodating such moral differences in constructive discourse may seem absurd or objectionable.

Let us suppose that two individuals, Samantha and Sue, have a disagreement about abortion. Samantha thinks that there is no reason to regard the foetus as being morally considerable; she thinks it has too few of the properties which beings of moral worth are supposed to possess. Sue thinks that a human life is itself of value and deserves moral consideration whatever stage it is in. Let us suppose that the views of these individuals have been thoroughly criticised and reflected upon. This means that each from her own point of view has reason to think her position is right: she can give good reasons for her point of view which the other has to acknowledge are rational reasons. She has reflected on it in relation to her experiences, the criticisms of others, and what she thinks is morally important; it can't be dismissed as prejudiced or ill-informed, as the result of an error of reasoning or a dogmatic ideological belief. So each has reason to think that the view of the other, though different from her own, is cogent.

Both accept the conclusion reached in Chapter 3, that ethical perspectives are limited, and judgments, however well-justified from an individual's perspective, are partial. This means that each has good reason to think that her view is probably not correct, however inclined she is to believe it. Since she aims to be a rational ethical agent, Samantha cannot suppose that abortion is wrong just because she has reason, from her own point of view, to think that it is; and Sue cannot suppose that she is right to think that abortion is allowable. However, each also has reason to believe that her position, though partial, is also rational and, indeed, insightful, and thus that any attempt to determine the right view about abortion must take it into account. These meta-ethical considerations motivate them to engage in constructive discourse: to attempt to incorporate what is insightful in each position into a conclusion that both can accept. The conclusion has to be constructed because there is no transcendent perspective from which they, or anyone else, can evaluate the positions and determine what is true.

To reach a constructed conclusion each will be prepared to make an 'accommodation' with the other but will put forward proposals that incorporate as much as possible of what she regards as important.

'Accommodation' in this context does not mean 'compromise' but a willing-ness to accept proposals which seem to embody insights from both positions. Sam proposes that abortion be morally permissible up to the time when a foetus becomes a creature capable of action and will. This criterion embodies some of what she thinks is important for moral considerability. To Sue this cut off point seems arbitrary and unacceptable. She proposes that abortion could be permitted in the very early stages of pregnancy when the fertilised cells are still capable of dividing to form more than one embryo. Human life, she reasons, is present before that stage (and from her point of view abortion at any stage still seems wrong), but she is willing to accept that there is a moral difference between human life and the life of a distinct human being. To Samantha this cut off point seems unreasonable. She thinks that the characteristics which make a being morally considerable appear much later in its development. She makes another proposal: that abortion be allowable up to the time when the foetus' nervous system, including its cere-bral cortex, has developed. The development of the brain and nervous system is significant, she reasons, because it is what gives a foetus the capa-bility of possessing morally considerable properties. Sue finds this position less arbitrary and thus more acceptable than Samantha's previous proposal. Having a nervous system of a particular kind, she reasons, is what makes an individual distinctly human.

Sue and Samantha have thus come to a conclusion which, in the opinion of both, incorporates better than any other proposal what each regards as morally important. This may not be the end of the matter. Sue or Samantha may not yet be satisfied that the position reached is as good as it can be. Sue may think, for example, that her view has not been given an equal weight, and if so will make another proposal or an amendment to a proposal. However, if the proposal she makes is worse as far as Samantha is concerned than it is better as far as she is concerned, then it is not acceptable, and she must try again, or acknowledge that the previous proposal is the dialogic equilibrium.

This example is artificial in a number of respects. First of all, it does not consider in sufficient detail the reasons each participant will have for her position and for (or against) the proposals made by herself and others. The judgments an individual makes about relation of her position to the proposals made in dialogue will depend on what exactly her position is and why she holds it. Judging a proposal is not, of course, something that only she can do. Since others understand, or can come to understand, her posi-tion, and her reasons for ranking proposals as she does, they are also in a position to make a judgment about how well she does this. A constructive discourse will have to allow discussion about the judgments of participants and will be able to criticise their reasons for ranking proposals as they do.

In presenting their positions and proposals, participants are not likely to confine themselves to the discussion of a single issue. The second reason why the example is over-simplified is that a discourse, whether critical or constructive, is likely to range over a number of related issues. Participants in a discourse will not merely be trying to reach a conclusion about abortion (even if that is the original motivation for the discussion). To deal with the issues that are bound to arise as soon as they offer reasons for their position, they will also have to consider other issues having to do with the value of life, and the proposals they make in constructive discourse will be designed to resolve as many of them as possible.

The third, and most important, reason why the example is artificial is that the participants are only considering two out of all the incompatible but cogent positions on abortion and related issues. Since the range of positions which figure in their attempt to reach equilibrium is far from complete, they have no reason to believe that their agreed conclusion is the right position on abortion. They do not even have good reason to think that their equilibrium position is *better* than either of their original positions. Participants will not be justified in regarding a conclusion as true unless they have reason to believe that they have taken *all* relevant positions into account.

Since the imagined dialogue between Sue and Samantha is a long distance from a real constructive discourse, there is plenty of room for doubts about the nature of the procedure and its outcome. Some critics will doubt whether constructive discourse is capable of reaching any conclusion at all. Aren't there likely to be irresolvable controversies among participants about what counts as the dialogic equilibrium? If this turns out to be the case, then ethical collectivism fails, after all, to solve the problem of disagreement. Or maybe participants will come up with more than one non-equivalent proposal, each an equally good candidate for the equilibrium position and will not be capable of deciding which they should accept. Or worse, the procedure itself may be incapable of reaching an unambiguous result. The requirement that cogent views should be treated equally may be compatible with more than one procedure and each may lead us to different (non-equivalent) conclusions. Let us look more closely at each of these threats to constructive discourse.

The method of constructive discourse

Constructive discourse is a procedure for non-ideal agents. This means that it may be possible in principle for participants to reach one and only one result, and yet for contingent reasons they do not do so. They may fail to agree on a proposal or may not be able to decide between more than one equally plausible proposal because one or more of them is not certain about how a proposal should be ranked, or is not able to appreciate properly a particular proposal, or because no one has yet come up with a proposal that resolves their difficulties. These and other failings are not peculiar to constructive discourse. If we have reason to suppose that agreement is possible then participants can hope that they will eventually be able to over-come their disagreements or at least make progress in doing so.

However, this hope could turn out to be unreasonable. There is no way of ruling out the possibility that participants will not be able to reach agree-ment however hard they try and however rational they are. Since participants in constructive discourse are ethical collectivists – since they accept the idea of ethical rationality which motivates the search for a constructed conclusion – they will not dissent from a proposal simply because it is different from their own position. However, they are justified in refusing to accept a proposal which ignores their concerns or fails to incor-porate any of the considerations they regard as important. A participant is not required to accept a result just because it is what he regards as the best of a bad lot. Ethical collectivism cannot rule out the possibility that every proposal ranked highly by one group of people in a discourse will be ranked very low by another, and that all attempts to find an acceptable equilibrium position will fail. Ethical differences of opinion could be so extreme that no conclusion which all can accept can be constructed in discourse. If this happens several possibilities will have to be considered. It could be the case that not all positions considered are cogent. Participants will want to engage in critical discourse to determine whether this is so. It could happen that there is a correct proposal but participants have so far failed to find it. It could also mean that relativism of a certain kind is true, a possibility that will seem more likely if the disagreements can be attributed to cultural differences. If cultural relativism turns out to be true then failure to reach a conclusion in such cases should not be blamed on the procedure. It is simply the way things are, ethically speaking. The truth of cultural relativism would also not prevent people of each culture from reaching a conclusion accept-able to them in constructive discourse.

Much the same thing can be said about cases where participants reach more than one conclusion each of which is acceptable as an equilibrium position, or where participants are not sure what position to accept. The problem may be resolved by critical discussion or by a new proposal. But it may not. It could be the case, as Susan Wolf suggests, that some ethical issues have no unique solution. If so, constructive discourse cannot be blamed for not finding one in those cases.[2]

Ethical collectivism would be seriously undermined, however, if failure to agree or to reach a unique conclusion were the consequence of ambiguity or vagueness in the procedure itself. A procedure is vague if individuals are unable to determine how to fulfil its requirements: if they are either unable to get definite results by following its directions or they can do so only by making arbitrary decisions. A procedure is ambiguous if either its require-ments are compatible with a number of methods which can yield incompatible results, or its prescribed method can be interpreted in incom-patible ways. If a procedure is ambiguous then the decision about how to use it, and thus what result to accept, has to be an arbitrary one. Ambiguity is thus a particular way in which a procedure can be vague.

A little bit of vagueness is not enough to condemn a procedure. Vagueness is something that we sometimes have to live with, and whether it is unacceptable depends on its context and how systematic or incurable it is. We cannot expect to achieve the same precision in science as in mathematics or in ethics as in science, and should not be unduly dismayed when our criteria cannot provide us with a definite answer to a difficult question. It is no failure of rationality if we are sometimes uncertain about how to rank an ethical proposal or how to assess the ranking of another individual. It would be fatal, as far as the acceptability of a procedure is concerned, if we could seldom or never do this, or if we did not know, in many cases, what we should do to resolve our uncertainty or to deal with the inconsistencies in our ranking.

Let us say, for example, that I am inclined to rank proposal A as better than proposal B, and proposal B better than proposal C, but feel that proposal C is better than proposal A. If a procedure provided us with no non-arbitrary way of dealing with this inconsistency in ranking, then it would be unacceptably vague. However, there is no reason to believe that participants in discourse cannot in most cases resolve ranking problems. For the ranking of proposals, and other decisions made by participants in discourse, is not merely a matter of feeling. Their decisions are not unchallengeable. They will have reasons for their judgments, and when they are inclined to rank inconsistently, they (and others) can critically examine and reassess these reasons and/or the ethical judgments on which their position is based. If it turns out that an individual's ethical position is inconsistent, then he should be able to determine why this is so: whether he has made a mistake in reasoning or judgment or whether he is really in more than one mind about an ethical matter (in which case his inconsistency in ranking will be treated in a different way).

As far as the reasoning of individuals is concerned, constructive discourse does not seem to be open to the accusation of vagueness, at least no more than any other ethical procedure. But constructive discourse is a collective procedure, and special critical attention needs to be focused on those aspects which require group decision-making. For the methods collectives use to make decisions are notoriously subject to ambiguity. If the requirement that a dialogic equilibrium be reached from cogent ethical positions can be satisfied in a number of incompatible and equally plausible ways then the 'procedure' of constructive discourse is hopelessly ambiguous. But even if there is (apparently) only one procedure which satisfies the requirement in a plausible way, it may turn out that this method yields incompatible results depending on how exactly it is applied. The problem is not that no decision can be made using an ambiguous procedure. A group may decide for political reasons to interpret a procedure in a particular way and abide by the results. Ethical collectivism aims to provide a means for arriving at justified ethical belief, and not merely an acceptable way of ending conflict. A defence of constructive discourse must therefore not only establish that there is an unambiguous method for constructing a conclusion. It must give us good reason to think that this procedure is a plausible means of reaching the truth of the matter – that it is defensible from an epistemological point of view.

This defence is best conducted by examining some methods that might be proposed for conducting a constructive discourse and determining why they succeed or fail to achieve a result that the participants can regard as true. Consider, for example, the proposal that the conclusion reached by constructive discourse should be determined by voting. Participants would, perhaps, rank ethical positions presented to discourse in order of preference, and the proposal which receives the most votes when the ordering of the preferences is taken into account is the one they are supposed to accept. (There are different techniques for counting preferences, so this method, as described, is itself ambiguous.) Equal treatment is interpreted to require that each position be a 'candidate' for choice and that each participant has an equal entitlement to vote and have his vote counted.

This method clearly will not do. For one thing, it does not do justice to the reason why ethical positions are being considered in constructive discourse. The position that wins the poll will do so because it is the most popular or the least unpopular. And a position which is not popular at all, which is outside the mainstream of ethical views, has no hope of being the one accepted. But the less popular positions as well as the more popular ones are supposed to be regarded as equally cogent. The popularity of a proposal cannot give it more cogency. Each position is a well-tested result coming from a particular perspective – a point of view which participants in discourse ought to regard as insightful, even though it is different from their own. This is why it is necessary that constructive discourse aim to reach a dialogic equilibrium in which each position has been accorded equal weight. So someone whose view is less popular can rightly complain that the proposal which wins the poll will be closer to the ethical positions of the majority than it is to his position; that his position, though equally cogent, has not been equally regarded. The poll thus fails to treat positions as equal in the right kind of way.

Another problem with the voting procedure for reaching a conclusion in discourse is that if we accept that a position is insightful, that the content of this position, though partial, is germane to the truth, then it should in some way be incorporated into the more impartial conclusion that is supposed to be the result of discourse. The poll does not do this. It simply selects one of the positions as the conclusion of discourse, and what the others say doesn't count. Since this conclusion is merely one of the partial positions presented to discourse it doesn't deserve to be regarded as an ethical truth. The situation would not be significantly better if the participants in discourse voted on proposals made in discourse rather than on the positions individuals bring to discourse. The winner would be the most popular proposal and not something that we can reasonably regard as true.

Making a decision by taking a vote is clearly not compatible with a procedure which aims to reach an dialogic equilibrium. But is there only one possible method of achieving an equilibrium among positions considered in constructive discourse? I have suggested that participants in constructive discourse should collect a complete set of cogent positions on related ethical issues (a set of positions as complete as it can be at that time and place) and construct a conclusion by considering all of these proposals together. Since all of the positions are considered at the same time in discourse this procedure could be labelled the 'method of synchronic comparison'. But someone might recommend that participants use instead a 'method of diachronic comparison'. This would require that they begin by considering two cogent positions and reach a constructed conclusion (as imagined in the abortion example). They then consider together this conclusion and a third cogent position and arrive at another constructed conclusion, and so on. Diachronic comparison, it might be argued, is not only a plausible way of reaching a result, but it is also more realistic. Participants in discourse are not required to start with a complete set of ethical positions. They can take into account positions as they encounter them by comparing them to the result they have already achieved.

However, the method of synchronic comparison and the method of diachronic comparison are not likely to come to the same conclusions. Let us suppose that a constructed conclusion is a view midway between the two most extreme positions (though this will not inevitably be the case, as I will explain below). Suppose also that there are just three cogent views about a particular set of issues, two extreme (right and left) and one moderate. Given these assumptions, synchronic comparison of these views will reach a constructed conclusion which is more or less identical with the middle view. A diachronic comparison between the left extreme and the moderate position will yield a position left of centre. This new position when compared with the right extreme will yield a view right of centre – that is, a position which is not likely to be similar to the position reached by synchronic comparison.

Let us suppose, for example, that there are only three cogent positions concerning how we should treat animals: that no animal should be exploited in any way, whether for meat or other products (L); that there is nothing morally wrong with exploiting animals for meat and other products, though it is wrong to torture animals for pleasure (R); and that animals can only be exploited for food and other products in cases where this creates important human benefits and considerable effort is made to minimise suffering (M). According to the assumption made, the constructed conclusion that results from taking into account all of these positions is going to be similar to M. But suppose we instead proceed in a diachronic way by first arriving at a conclusion by considering R and M, and then making an accommodation between that conclusion and L. In discussing proposals for accommodating R and M participants will be assuming that some uses of animals are allowable and are thus likely to end up with a conclusion which reflects this. Let us suppose that they conclude that exploitation of animals is all right only if it produces *some* benefits and if *some* effort is made to minimise suffering (MR). Now they are forced to confront L, a position they have so far not considered. The method of diachronic comparison requires that they treat both L and MR as cogent positions, and this means that they must be accorded equal weight. The method also requires that they not consider R (since this has already been done). But since L is an extreme position, proposals for accommodating it (when MR is the only other position under consideration) are going to be closer to it than they are to R. After all, MR concedes that exploitation is problematic and now it seems that at issue are what moral restrictions should be put on how we use animals even when doing so is beneficial to us. Because of the weight of L, high ranking proposals are unlikely to be similar to M. Participants are more likely to end up with a conclusion which puts heavier restrictions on animal exploitation – perhaps one which allows us to use animals only if the benefits they provide are *essential* to us.

Moreover, the method of diachronic comparison is itself ambiguous. What result we end up with is likely to depend on whether we start by comparing the middle with the left extreme or the middle with the right extreme or the extremes with each other. If, for example, we start by comparing L (the position that all exploitation of animals is wrong) with M (the position that exploitation is justified only by important benefits), and regard the result as a cogent position which should be considered alongside R (the position that exploitation is allowable), the final conclusion is likely to be different from M, and it is also not guaranteed to be the same as the conclusion reached by the first use of diachronic comparison. So if the method of diachronic comparison turns out to be the right method for constructive discourse (or one of the right methods), then it would be absurd to regard any conclusion of discourse as a 'truth', however loosely this term is used.

The diachronic approach is clearly unacceptable for methodological reasons. However, it is important to note that it is also unsatisfactory from an epistemological of view. It only appears to make sense because we are accustomed to thinking about moral development from a monological point of view. If an individual who has reached a conclusion from his own experience and reflection has to take into account a moral position which he has never before considered, he will test it in the way described in the Chapter 4, and may as a result modify his views. He then takes for granted the cogency of his new position until he is forced to confront a new challenge. The development of an individual's moral point of view is diachronic in the sense that it is a progress from positions which he now sees as unsatisfactory to a position which he has reason to believe is more adequate. In this progression the only position that counts is the one he now has. The previous ones have been discarded and can be ignored. A conclusion arrived at in constructive discourse, on the other hand, cannot be regarded as the end point of such a diachronic development. Its existence does not licence us to discard, and henceforth ignore, the positions which were taken into account in its construction.

Consider for example what would happen if participants in the constructive discourse about the treatment of animals were to discover a cogent position which they had not before considered. Let us suppose that they have reached a constructed conclusion taking into account only positions which presuppose that exploitation of animals is morally allowable (at least in some cases). Now for the first time they encounter individuals who think that all exploitation of animals, even for such things as milk and eggs, is wrong. Let us assume that they cannot dismiss this position as being dogmatic, illogical, biased or ill-informed, and so have to regard it as a cogent position. It would not be satisfactory if they took the conclusion they have already reached in constructive discourse as the starting point for their consideration of the new position. For the fact that the conclusion was reached before the new position was known not only calls this conclusion into question, but also calls into question the way it was constructed. When participants arrived at their constructed conclusion, they assumed that they were considering the complete set of relevant cogent positions on the treatment of animals. The proposals that they made for accommodating them, and the reasons for their proposals presupposed this belief. When they realise that this assumption is false, they not only have to rethink their own cogent positions in the light of the new position and the arguments for it, but they have to consider it alongside all of the others when making and arguing for proposals for a constructed conclusion. Participants in the discourse about animals will want to consider how the arguments given for L relate to those given for R, as well as for MR and all other positions. They will have these comparisons and reasons in mind when they make proposals for a constructed conclusion. The existence of a new position transforms the ground on which constructive discourse takes place, and it therefore requires construction to begin anew.

The problems associated with diachronic comparison make it clear that a distinction has to be made between cogent positions and proposals for a constructed conclusion. A diachronic comparison requires us to treat a conclusion reached in one constructive discourse as a cogent position in a later discourse. No distinction is made between a constructed conclusion, or a proposal for a constructed conclusion, and the ethical positions offered to discourse by participants. It is assumed that proposals and positions have the same epistemological status. This is a mistake – rather similar in kind to the mistake of confusing data with hypotheses for explaining them. An ethical *position* is justified by the experiences and reflections of an individual. A *proposal* is justified by whether and to what degree it answers to the concerns of individuals who hold different but equally cogent ethical positions. The conclusion reached by discourse is the most satisfactory proposal. Diachronic comparison puts on an equal footing propositions which occupy different epistemological levels.

There are additional reasons for thinking that a failure to make this distinction leads to unacceptable epistemological consequences. If a conclusion reached by one discourse is regarded as a position in the next, the views of participants in discourse will not be treated equally in the required way. Let us assume once again that there are three positions (left (L), right (R), and moderate (M)) and that the conclusion accepted by a discourse will be midway between the positions considered. Participants first consider L and M and settle on the proposal LM, midway between L and M. They then consider LM and R and construct a conclusion which is closer to R than it is to L. But this means that the position R is being given more weight in reaching the final result than are the positions L and M (as the case of the discourse about animals shows). However, there is no epistemological reason for this favourable treatment, and participants who hold L and M can reasonably object to the procedure, and holders of R and M could make the same objection if the order of consideration were reversed. The reason why the method of diachronic comparison is unsatisfactory is because it favours proposals it happens to consider later over proposals considered earlier. The order of consideration counts, and there is no good reason why it should do so.

The method of diachronic comparison is inadequate because it fails to treat equally positions with an equal epistemological status. Only a method which requires that all positions be considered together, and does not confuse positions with proposals, is going to answer to the epistemological reasons for holding a constructive discourse. Synchronic comparison is the appropriate method for constructive discourse. But what is this method exactly? A critic might complain that there is no clear or unambiguous way of arriving at a conclusion from a complete set of equally cogent ethical positions.

One reason for thinking that no meaningful result can be obtained from a synchronic comparison of positions is motivated by the idea of an equilibrium as a midpoint. If we picture the positions represented in discourse as points distributed randomly in a space, then there is not likely to be any point in that space which is midway between all of them. Given that this is so, it makes no sense for participants in discourse to seek an equilibrium.

However, there are a number of problems with the spatial analogy which motivates this objection. One of them is that the equilibrium point is imagined to be another point in the same space. A dialogic equilibrium is not another ethical position with the same status as the positions represented in discourse. It occupies a different 'space'. It would be better to picture the equilibrium as the external focal point for points in a plane. More important, it is wrong to think of a dialogic equilibrium as equidistant from *all* positions. Participants in discourse are trying to arrive at a conclusion which incorporates as much as possible of what each participant regards as ethically important. The result may be a conclusion which is closer to some positions represented in discourse than to others. It may turn out to be identical to one of these positions.

Does this mean that constructive discourse gives unequal weight to the positions considered? If, for example, participants compare L, R and M and settle on a proposal identical in content to M, are they favouring the moderate position? Once again it is important to distinguish between positions and proposals. The participants adopt the proposal M not because they have given more weight to position M than to positions R and L, but because when every position is taken into account M, considered as a proposal, seems most satisfactory, or least unsatisfactory. Those who hold the position M are not assumed to be more insightful than any other participant in discourse. They have no reason to claim epistemological superiority. It simply turned out that they happened to be right. This is not something that they or anyone else could have determined prior to constructive discourse. Before discourse they had no more reason to think their view was right than did those who held other cogent positions.

It is also a mistake to think that a successful proposal is inevitably going to be identical or similar to the moderate proposal (though I have made this assumption for the sake of simplicity). The results of discourse need not be so conservative. It may turn out that the most satisfactory proposal, the one that best incorporates the ethical concerns of the participants, will be different from any of the particular positions considered in discourse. For what is important to the participants is not merely their positions, but the perceptions and reasons which justify these positions, and it is possible to imagine that the proposal which best incorporates the points of view which lie behind their positions is very different from the position they presented to constructive discourse. (The term 'dialogic equilibrium' is thus somewhat misleading.) Suppose that those trying to reach a conclusion about the treatment of animals give as reasons for their cogent positions views about the value of life. Suppose also that the proposal which best incorporates the ideas and feelings concerning this value is one that regards all creatures with a point of view as having value in their own right. By implication this would support a strong proposal concerning the treatment of animals, one likely to be much closer to L than it is to R.

There is clearly no formula for arriving at a proposal in constructive discourse – any more than there is an algorithm for discovering a scientific hypothesis. Once a proposal is made there is a procedure for determining whether it should be accepted or rejected, a procedure which, as we have seen, depends on participants being able to compare and rank this proposal with others. However, participants will never be sure that the proposal they have settled on is better than any possible proposal. Another, better one may some day be discovered. The work of constructive discourse, like other kinds of epistemological labour, is never finished.

There are other contingencies which can upset the conclusion reached by a constructive discourse. Confidence in the correctness of the result depends upon participants having reason to believe that all cogent positions are represented. This may turn out not to be so. New positions are likely to make their appearance as time goes by; participants may eventually decide that they were wrong about the cogency or lack of cogency of some of the positions in critical discourse. When this happens the method of synchronic comparison requires that every position be considered together, and that a new conclusion be constructed from the ground up. For it is possible that the new positions will cause participants to reassess their own points of view and thus change the positions they bring to discourse, or at least these new views may require that different kinds of proposals be made in constructive discourse. As a result, the conclusion they reach after they take into account new positions may be significantly different from the one they reached before.

A position or proposal is not supposed to be more or less privileged because it is considered earlier or later than other positions or proposals. A critic might point out that all positions and proposals cannot literally be examined together. Participants will have to consider them in some order, and how can we be sure that the particular order that they adopt will not affect the results that they get? This objection, it seems to me, confuses temporal order with logical ordering. When the position C is introduced into discourse it can be compared with position A and B, and a judgment can be made by participants about whether the existence of C gives them a reason for reassessing A or B or proposals hitherto made for accommodating A and B. Since new positions or proposals require that every conclusion so far reached be re-examined, the temporal order of their consideration or discovery should not make a difference to the results.

This doesn't mean that ethical inquiry cannot be affected in any way by the contingencies of its history. By considering existing positions and examining and arguing about proposals that happen to come up in discourse, participants are developing a particular overview of ethical matters. This outlook may well affect in subtle ways their treatment of new positions and new proposals. It is not merely ethics that is likely to be affected by the history of inquiry. Even science may have been shaped by contingent events in its history. If its history had been different – if scientists had had different interests or had made different discoveries or discovered some things earlier or later – then theories of science might have been different from what they now are. Reflection on such contingencies and their possible results does not prevent scientists from regarding existing theories as knowledge, as what they are justified in regarding as true, and similar reflections should also not prevent us from regarding the conclusions of discourse as right or true.

Monology reconsidered

There is no reason to believe that the procedures used by participants in constructive discourse are ambiguous or vague. There is no reason to think that participants who accept the requirements of discourse will not in most cases be able to construct a conclusion that all can endorse. This means that there is a viable non-monological method of making ethical decisions, and if my earlier arguments are correct, it is the *only* viable means of making most ethical decisions. Some critics will continue to dispute the idea that ethical decision-making is or can be non-monological: some because they persist in thinking that an ethical decision-procedure must be monological or nonsense; others because they think that ethical decision-making is in principle monological, even though individuals like us are not capable of reaching true conclusions for ourselves.

The first objection is simply stated. If an individual is to be justified in accepting the conclusion of a constructive discourse then he or she must be in a position to regard that conclusion as correct. This means that he must be able to assess the conclusion in the light of his own understanding of what is good or bad, right or wrong. So there is no alternative to monology.

This objection is also simply answered. A participant in discourse must indeed have good reasons for accepting a conclusion. But it is question-begging to assume that his reasons must derive from his own ethical point of view. An individual has good reason to accept the results of discourse if and only if he knows that all of the requirements of critical and constructive discourse have been satisfied. A non-monological ethical decision-procedure depends, as I have pointed out, on a monological agreement about the nature of ethical rationality and the requirements of discourse. However, a rational agent will not presume that he is, or can be, an authority on what is ethically true (given the kind of creature he is).

The second objection requires that we look more carefully at what ethical collectivists mean when they say that an individual cannot by herself determine what is true. Claims about what is possible in principle, as I have said (in Chapter 1), can be interpreted as claims about what *we* are capable of doing; or alternatively, as claims about the capabilities of agents who do not suffer from our limitations. As a non-ideal ethical agent, I have good reason to think that I will not be able to reach a sound ethical conclusion by myself, even with the benefit of the criticisms of others. This does not mean that it is impossible for an ideally rational agent to perform this feat. I have argued, after all, that it is possible for individuals to understand the positions and perspectives of others, including those who have contrary opinions. It is also possible for an individual to understand why another individual makes a particular proposal in discourse or why he ranks proposals in the way he does. It is possible for an individual to come up with a proposal for reconciling points of view and to assess judgments made about that proposal. Given that all this is so, it must be possible in principle for an individual to comprehend all relevant points of view and to construct from them a dialogic equilibrium. The task would be much the same, though more difficult, than the construction by an individual of a conclusion from his own inconsistent positions. If he can do the former, then what, aside from the difficulty and complexity of the task, prevents him from doing the latter? Discourse and collective decision-making, the critic could argue, may in practice be indispensable. We can't suppose that any one of us is capable of appreciating all points of view or making the best possible proposal. But since it is *in principle* possible for an agent to do this, monology is vindicated: an individual using his own resources and judgment can arrive at a correct ethical conclusion.

An ethical collectivist can and should admit that it is in principle possible for an individual to do the work of constructive discourse. This does not make ethical reasoning monologic or do away with the need for collective decision-making. For the ideal ethical reasoner must himself take into account all relevant points of view and reach an accommodation between them. He must carry on a dialogue with himself in which he takes in turn each possible position and considers the issues in question from that particular point of view. He must make proposals and assess them from each of these points of view in turn, and aim for a conclusion which is as good as possible judged from each point of view. The ideal reasoner does not replace constructive discourse; he incorporates it.

The reasoning of the ideal individual is not monological reasoning. It is not the same as the reasoning of the scientist who takes into account the hypotheses of others and then makes his own considered judgment about what is true. The scientist assesses the new hypotheses from his point of view; he either accepts or rejects a hypothesis depending on how well it accounts for the evidence as he understands it and how well it fits in with other things that he believes to be true. If he accepts the hypothesis, this means that he has revised or given up some of his old beliefs; he has changed his point of view. In the case of constructive discourse, whether this is carried on by a group of people or in the head of the ideal ethical judge, points of view do not disappear or become altered by their exposure to other points of view. If they have survived critical discourse then there is no reason why they should. Agreement is reached through construction rather than revision of a position or a point of view.

The ideal constructer is in a position similar to the person earlier described who is in two minds about how he should resolve an ethical problem (the situation which I imagined Sartre's student to be in). This predicament exists, I have argued, because an ethical agent can have more than one perspective, and from these perspectives he may sometimes make different and conflicting judgments about particular issues. For an agent in this position, the way of resolving the problem is not to appeal to the perceptions and generalisations that depend on these perspectives (since this will not resolve the problem) but to construct a conclusion which takes into account the reasoning behind both positions and gives each equal weight. The ideal constructer has to perform this task not just for positions which come from two different perspectives, but for all the cogent positions concerning the issue in question.

An appeal to what an ideal agent could do does not support the view that ethical reasoning is really monological. It does require a more precise account of what non-monological reasoning is. We will have to allow that an ideal agent can by means of his own epistemological resources come to a correct conclusion about what is right or wrong. For his resources include his ability to appreciate and take into account all other possible positions. What he cannot do (if he is enough like us so that his reasoning is intelligible to us) is to determine from his own ethical perspective, by means of his own experiences and reflections, what is right or wrong. His perspectives are multiple, and there is no transcendent perspective from which his positions can be judged. The conclusion of non-monological reasoning, whether this reasoning is conducted by one person or by a collective, depends for its acceptability upon how it is constructed, whether it incorporates better than any alternative all cogent positions on a related set of issues – and not on how plausible it seems to a particular individual from his own point of view.

The ethical collectivist claims that these constructed conclusions are true, at least that we are justified in believing that they are correct. Even those prepared to accept that many ethical decisions can and must be made by non-monological means may continue to reject this claim. They may be happy to regard constructive discourse as an appropriate means of making political decisions in cases where people have different ethical points of view. But they will resist regarding these conclusions as right or true. In some countries institutional decision-making on bio-ethical issues, like the permissibility of experiments on human embryos, has been determined or influenced by ethics committees made up of people who represent the main points of view on the matter. These representatives are expected to reach some sort of accommodation with each other that they can present to legislators or the managers of institutions. They are not required to think that the compromise position is *morally* right. Each can believe that the committee has made the right political decision, and yet continue to believe that his own position is morally superior. Why should participants in a constructive discourse think any differently?

It may help to point out the differences between constructive discourse and the nature and procedure of ethics committees. Views represented on ethics committees are generally not all the positions on a particular issue that exist, but the opinions of the people who count, politically speaking: those who have a vested interest in the institution or who are too powerful to ignore. Many of these views have not been thoroughly subjected to criticism. The committee has to accommodate them even when many of its members do not regard them as cogent. Moreover, the committee is supposed to make a decision about a specific matter in a very limited time. It cannot discuss all related matters or consider all relevant proposals. So it is not surprising that participants do not feel compelled to accept the result as true. However, the more rigorous the procedure of an ethics committee becomes, the more it tries to include all relevant views, the more it insists upon rational procedure, the more similar it is to constructive discourse and the less reason we have for thinking that its conclusion is merely a political compromise.

The idea that constructive discourse is really about the accommodations individuals with conflicting opinions must make in order to reach an agreement about what should be permitted or forbidden in their society may also be encouraged by the examples and terminology I have used. Out of monological habit it is easy to suppose that the agreement between Samantha and Sue about abortion and the conclusion reached in the debate about the treatment of animals are agreements about what ought to be permitted given that individuals have irreconcilable ideas about what is right. The fact that I have used 'accommodation' to describe what the participants in discourse are trying to do is likely to confirm this impression of what discourse really achieves. However, if my account of moral judgments is correct – if they are limited and partial and at the same time insightful and rational – and if constructive discourse is a rational procedure for determining the truth of the matter (as I have been arguing), then what discourse achieves is not merely pragmatic agreement, and individuals who have reached a conclusion through constructive discourse are not entitled to hang onto their original ethical views. On the contrary, they have reason to believe that their collectively arrived at conclusion is right.

Ontological implications

The conclusion of a properly conducted constructive discourse deserves to be accepted. But does it really count as true? I have been assuming that what passes appropriate epistemological tests deserves to be called true. However, there is truth and Truth. Ethical collectivism is not an ontological theory, and it is not in the business of taking a stand on ontological matters. Nevertheless, it is reasonable to want to know whether it entails or is entailed by, supports or is supported by, any particular ontological position.

Some ontological positions are clearly incompatible with ethical collectivism. The theory is incompatible with reductionist views which identify ethical responses wholly or in part with non-rational emotional reactions or with the non-rational decisions or commitments of agents. The question remains as to whether ethical collectivism naturally allies itself with a realist or a non-realist view of ethical value. I have claimed that ethical collectivism is compatible with both of these ontological positions. Not everyone is going to believe this. Many will think that ethical collectivism is the epistemological counterpart of the view, often called constructivism, that ethical positions are what we fabricate in order to deal with our interactions with each other. So understood, ethics is an institution rather like the law, and ethical reasoning should be likened to making law and not to discovering an empirical truth. The reason why someone might think that the metaphysics of ethical collectivism must be non-realist is not simply the coincidence of terminology – the very idea of a 'constructed' conclusion – but also the way in which this construction takes place.

Ronald Dworkin argues in 'Justice and rights' that moral theories which presuppose an objective moral reality distinguish themselves from constructivist theories in their aims and methods. The former, those which adopt the 'natural model', proceed from the assumption that moral intuitions are accurate observations of reality. So if an individual has opposing moral intuitions, he has to put this inconsistency aside for the time being and hope that a theory will come along which reconciles his data. He does not give up the belief that his intuitions are an insight into the nature of reality (unless he finds an independent reason to doubt them). On the other hand, constructivists, Dworkin says, are motivated by the imperative of finding a moral position acceptable to people in a community. They will be prepared to jettison some of their intuitive convictions for the sake of reaching this consensus. The constructivist model is 'a model that someone might propose for the governance of a community each of whose members has strong convictions that differ, though not too greatly, from the convictions of others' (Dworkin 1977: 163). The method which Rawls employs in order to arrive at a theory of justice is, Dworkin argues, an application of the constructive model. This suggests that the epistemological method which Daniels calls wide reflective equilibrium, a method which I recommend for critical discourse, presupposes constructivist metaphysics.

Goldman recommends the constructive method for the whole of ethics for reasons very similar to Dworkin's.

> In ethics, there appear to be many incompatible normative systems that are internally coherent, that meet all relevant inductive criteria,

and that are not only consistent with all observational data, but equally plausible (to different rational evaluators) given the data.

(Goldman 1988: 174)

If we are to reach an agreement about what is right or wrong, he argues, we must construct moral theories in much the same way as the law is constructed. Ethical method is similar to legal method – not to the method of science – and though it is proper, in his view, to call ethical propositions true, an interpretation of what this means should be a non-realist one. Constructive discourse, so it might be thought, is an example of the constructive model in its aim and its method, and if so, it would be a mistake to think that a realist could accept it.

However, this identification is mistaken. Constructive discourse is motivated not by the desire to reach a public consensus, but by an epistemological thesis. According to ethical collectivism, the judgments of individuals are inevitably partial. This is why individuals are not entitled to regard their moral intuitions as accurate ethical observations. They enter into a constructive discourse, not for the sake of reaching a publicly endorsable agreement, but because this is the only way of making a true judgment. Ethical collectivists do not have to be realists, but there is no reason, as far as their theory is concerned, why they should not be.

Ethical collectivism does not imply the truth, or even the probability, of realism. It does show how one serious objection to realism can be met. One problem for realists, as Goldman notes, is the apparent unresolvability of ethical disagreements. If rational ethical agents cannot manage to converge on something they can all recognise as true, then, so long as there is no alternative to monology, it seems reasonable to conclude that there is no fact of the matter as far as ethics is concerned. For this reason ethical theorists find the force of non-realism difficult to resist. Ethical collectivism not only provides a way of resolving disagreement. It allows us to think of our ethical observations as insightful, though partial, perceptions of reality. Ethical collectivism is realism's last best hope.

It might be objected that the support ethical collectivism provides for realism is undermined by the admission that relativism of a certain kind can be true. I have admitted that only those who accept the ideas of ethical rationality embodied in ethical collectivist procedures are committed to accepting its conclusions, and I have allowed that a failure of individuals to reach a conclusion by dialogic means can provide support for a relativist view. However, neither of these concessions to relativism poses a serious problem for realism. The recognition that people could have different ideas about ethical rationality is no more a challenge to realist ethics (as I have argued) than the existence of magical reasoning about the world is to scientific realism. In ethics as in science we have no non-question-begging way of dismissing other 'rationalities'. But this does not prevent us from making

115

claims about the nature of reality. Neither does the threat of radical disagreement. For if people have views that are *so* far apart, then it is reasonable to regard them as having a different conception of the ethical.

Whether realism is right or not, the conclusions of constructive discourse deserve to be regarded as 'true'. Acceptance of realism would only eliminate the scare quotes. My defence of ethical collectivism is more or less complete. Nevertheless, there are bound to be rational, sensitive individuals who strongly resist the very idea that a collective can determine what an individual should believe or how he should act. In Chapter 6 I will discuss the reasons conscientious agents might have for this resistance and how their concerns can be met.

Part III

ETHICAL COLLECTIVISM AND ETHICAL AGENCY

6

CONSCIENCE, AUTHENTICITY AND COLLECTIVE DECISION-MAKING

People often say that it is important for individuals to live according to their moral convictions. We are supposed to march to our own drummer, listen to our conscience, stand up for what we believe in our hearts is right. Some of the greatest heroes of our culture are the individuals of integrity who said, 'Here I stand' and were not moved from their position by the persuasion or threats of others: the religious non-conformists who insisted on following their own idea of what is right; the humanitarians who opposed slavery long before this was a popular thing to do; the feminists who argued in the face of ridicule and denunciation that women ought to be accorded equal rights in social life; the Germans who recognised Nazism as an evil and did what they could to fight it. Those who believe in the importance of the 'inner voice' are likely to see ethical collectivism as a backward step for morality: as a doctrine that supports the domination of the group over the conscientious individual, undermines personal integrity, destroys the moral will, and makes it impossible for rebels and non-conformists to retain the courage of their convictions.

However, those who have the courage of their convictions include rabid racists and sexists, as well as religious fundamentalists and ideologues of all kinds. In fact, ideologues are more likely to be filled with passionate conviction than are reasonable people, who are prepared to think that they might be wrong. Even rebels, admirable for their courage, may in good conscience persecute unbelievers if the tables of power are turned. Righteousness, even in the pursuit of a good cause, is not a pretty sight. So those who think that ethical judgment can and should be rational have to reject the belief that conscience, that inner detector of good and evil, is an infallible guide, and anyone who insists that ethical beliefs be open to criticism has already distanced himself or herself from the idea that all those prepared to shout 'Here I stand' are moral heroes.

Nevertheless, most people, including moral philosophers, insist that in the end it is up to the individual to determine what is right – though they do not all have the same reasons for this belief. Some, especially those in the utilitarian tradition, believe that monological procedures are as adequate for moral reasoning as for other forms of theoretical and practical reasoning. Those in the Kantian tradition believe that moral judgment is essentially something that comes from within an individual as a product of his or her reason and will.[1] Kantian and utilitarian traditions have been taken to task by those who object to the abstract way in which an impersonal ethics conceives of moral agents or moral agency. But these opponents of abstract morality do not generally question the idea that the individual is the arbiter of what is morally right. On the contrary. These critics claim that any attempt by moral theory to transcend the ethical convictions which arise from a person's identity, relationships or idea of the good is mistaken. Ethical collectivists thus have to oppose both traditional monological ideas about moral agency and those critics of traditionalism who want to re-conceive the ethical as something tied to an individual's character, situation, or idea of the good.

I will first deal with objections to ethical collectivism which are likely to occur to many critics, whatever their views about ethical agents or ethical methods. These objections can themselves be answered, but they give rise to deeper and more difficult matters. For what is at stake in debates about ethical decision-making is not merely epistemological considerations, but views about individual identity and integrity, and the place and purpose of ethics in human life.

Ethics as practical reasoning

One obvious objection to the procedure required by ethical collectivism is that it does not properly appreciate the fact that ethics is a species of practical, rather than theoretical, reasoning: that it is supposed to provide guidance for ethical agents, to tell them what they ought to do in the particular situations they encounter. Actions are performed by individuals, the critic reminds us, and therefore individuals have to be the ones who make decisions about what to do. This cannot be delegated to a group.

The objection can be given a number of interpretations. It could simply be drawing attention to what could be called the 'quick response problem': the fact that many ethical decisions have to be made on the spot by the people who find themselves face to face with an ethical problem, and there is often no time for a lot of deliberation, let alone for consulting others or going through the procedure required by ethical collectivism. This problem does not by itself constitute an objection to ethical collectivism any more than it does to other ideas about ethical reasoning. People faced with an emergency have to do the best they can. They will be guided by their past experience and reflections, and, an ethical collectivist will insist, by the guidelines provided by constructive discourse. An individual who is required to respond quickly, has to acknowledge that she could make a mistake, that she might later come to the conclusion that she made the wrong decision. An ethical collectivist claims that the authority for such a judgment comes ultimately not from her own reflection on her deeds but from constructive discourse.

However, the difficulty posed by requirements of action can be understood not merely as a problem of responding quickly to situations requiring ethical judgment, but as a problem of interpretation. To act appropriately individuals have to be able to understand the situation that they are in. They have to interpret it as a situation calling for a certain kind of ethical judgment. And the ethical principle or guideline that they regard as relevant has to be interpreted by them so that it fits the situation. Ethical action is a form of art, it can be said, which requires of individuals that they have a feeling for a situation and for the guidelines they are applying. This kind of understanding is necessarily a possession of the individual agent. Critics of ethical collectivism will claim that this means that an individual must apply in her actions the principles or ideas that she has constructed for herself. The problem with ethical collectivism, according to this line of thought, is that the conclusions reached by constructive discourse are too remote from the individual's responses and her way of understanding the world she is in. Principles reached by accommodation with others do not belong to the ethical agent in the right kind of way. So how can she be expected to know how to interpret and apply them? She can only apply the results of discourse by interpreting them in her own way, and once she does this, they are no longer the conclusions that discourse arrived at.

The objection overstates the individuality of ethical interpretation. It seems to depend on the thesis that ethical judgments, even the meaning of the terms they use, are inherently subjective. If we don't make this assumption, then the idea that we don't or can't interpret moral principles or guidelines in the same way is less appealing. If it is possible for people to share ethical principles or ideas, or at least understand each other's positions – something that most moral philosophers assume to be the case – then ethical language must have a common meaning and interpretation. Nevertheless, ethical collectivism, more than most other views about ethical judgment, stresses the individuality of ethical response; it insists that individuals interpret and judge according to their own perspective. Is this compatible with supposing that they can interpret and apply in a common way guidelines that they have collectively arrived at?

Ethical collectivism does not suppose that the discourse which makes ethical decisions is a once and for all event – a kind of indoctrination programme for agents who are then sent out in the world to put guidelines into practice. Critical and constructive discourse are the means of making a connection between the personal and the impersonal, the judgments and interpretations of individuals and the impartial decisions of the collective. This interconnection, or dialectic, does not come to an end when the collective decision has been made. Individuals who have participated in a constructive discourse understand the decisions made; they have participated in making them. They have reached a common conclusion and know what reasoning went into reaching it. Those who did not participate in discourse can have it explained to them why a particular conclusion was reached and how it relates to their own view. So agents are not put in the position of having to interpret and apply commandments that they don't understand. Nevertheless, as they apply the guidelines to cases which were not envisioned or discussed in discourse, their interpretations, and hence their judgments, are likely to diverge. They will respond in their own individual way to the problems they face. They will encounter cases which cause them to doubt the conclusions reached by discourse. These new interpretations, criticisms and the reasons for them will be subject matter for a future discourse and will contribute to its process of collective decision-making.

Collective decisions are applied by individuals who have their own responses to the ethical world, and these responses are what individuals contribute to collective decision-making. There is no end to the process of ethical reasoning and no final pronouncements. The same could be said of any ethical decision-procedure. What is central to the ethical collectivist position is the insistence that collective decisions are authoritative. Individuals who put into practice ethical guidelines may find reasons for questioning the collective decision; they may interpret the guidelines in their own way and regard themselves as justified in doing so. But whether their objections are correct and how their interpretations are regarded is determined collectively in critical and constructive discourse – and not by the judgment of the individual, however well-motivated by her own point of view.

This reply might, however, encourage the critic to pose the following dilemma for ethical collectivism. A conscientious ethical agent will not only want to apply the principles arrived at in discourse, but she will also want to make the conclusion of constructive discourse into her own point of view. That is, she will want to change her way of perceiving so that making the right judgment becomes second nature. However, ethical collectivist method, as described in the Chapter 5, depends upon a distinction between cogent positions, judgments dependent on the point of view of individuals, and the constructed conclusions of discourse. If ethical agents themselves confuse these two things, if they make constructed conclusions into cogent positions, and represent them as such in the next constructive discourse, then the method of synchronic comparison has in fact become the method of diachronic comparison – with fatal results for claims made about the reliability of constructive discourse.

This objection depends upon an assumption that ethical collectivism denies. It supposes that there is a transcendent perspective, and that constructive discourse is merely the means by which an individual achieves transcendence. I have argued that this is false. Moreover, it does not accord with what we know about how perspectives are formed and changed. A perspective is shaped by experience and reflection on these experiences. It cannot be changed at will just because a person thinks that it would be a good idea to do so. There is no procedure available to an individual which would enable her to change her perspective so that judging according to the conclusions of constructive discourse becomes *her* way of moral perceiving.

Nevertheless, it could happen that a person's own way of judging does accord with, or comes to accord with, the conclusion reached through discourse. The conclusion of constructive discourse, as we have seen, can be identical to one of the cogent positions considered in it. For example, the cogent position that it is allowable to use animals for essential human purposes may turn out to be identical to the conclusion reached through construction. Through their own experiences and reflections some individuals may later come to have moral perceptions which support this judgment. However, this does not mean that these individuals have transcended their limitations or that their moral perspective is better than those of others. There is still a distinction between cogent positions, which are the result of individual perspectives, and the principles which individuals have reason to believe are right because they are the conclusions of constructive discourse.

However, this distinction, and the resulting epistemological gap between what individuals are inclined to believe when they consult their ethical perceptions and reflections and what they are justified in thinking is right, is likely to encourage another line of attack on ethical collectivism. Those who complain that ethical collectivism does not properly appreciate ethics as a form of practical reasoning might also be claiming that it does not provide an adequate account of moral motivation. Moral judgment is, after all, supposed to lead to action, and motivation for action has to come from the individual. The problem with ethical collectivism, according to these critics, is that it separates judgment from motivation more radically than do other theories about ethical rationality. Why should an individual be motivated to act according to collectively determined guidelines?

Ethical collectivism takes an 'externalist' view of moral motivation. It allows that an individual can know what is right and yet not be inclined to *do* the right. (It shares this view with many other moral theories.) This does not mean that it is at a loss to provide motivation for action. For one thing, the epistemological reasons an agent has for thinking that an action is right are themselves motivational. Scanlon (1982: 116) argues that moral motivation depends on individuals believing that their actions are in accordance with principles that others cannot reasonably reject. Ethical collectivism has a view about how to achieve this conviction and the motivation which goes along with it.

Another reason why ethical collectivists can claim to provide an account of moral motivation is that for them the motivation to do the right thing is not something that has to be supplied by lone individuals. Since action is up to the individual, she must be 'impelled' to action by the strength of her own will. But it would be a mistake to think that good willing depends merely on individual characteristics. Will is also conditioned and shaped by external factors, including the situation in which an individual acts and her relations to others. Her participation in discourse, direct or indirect, and the knowledge that all are committed to a collectively arrived at conclusion, will in itself be a powerful motivating force. Moral union makes us strong.

Moral responsibility

However, the idea that the voice of the collective is authoritative seems to come into conflict with a common understanding of ethics as a species of practical reasoning which requires that individuals make their own decisions and take responsibility for them. Raimond Gaita remarks that 'we cannot pass on our moral problems to someone else for a crack at their solution' (Gaita 1991: 105). We cannot delegate our moral decisions to others, as we can our financial and other practical business. We may take advice from friends, neighbours and counsellors about what we ought to do, but making the decision remains our responsibility, and Gaita thinks that this goes to show that ethical deliberation is essentially personal. Sartre can be understood as making a similar point. By requiring that individuals bow to the authority of the collective, ethical collectivism might be accused of offending against the requirement that individuals take responsibility for their own decisions and actions.

Ethical collectivists have no intention of denying that it is up to the individual to do the right thing – to make good decisions and carry them out. They simply have a particular idea about how an agent carries out her deliberative responsibilities. Being responsible involves contributing in one way or another to discourse and conscientiously carrying out the collective decision. It means that each ethical agent has to do what she can to ensure that the requirements of critical and constructive discourse are satisfied. An individual can legitimately be praised or blamed for fulfilling these requirements well or badly. I have allowed that not all individuals need to participate in discourse and that their point of view can be represented by others. Nevertheless, each individual has a responsibility for making sure that this happens, and that her point of view and the views of others are properly taken into account. If she conscientiously does this, then she cannot be accused of simply delegating decisions to others.

Ethical collectivism does not undermine individual responsibility. What it adds is a requirement of collective responsibility. Participants in discourse *share* a responsibility for ensuring that their procedures are rational, and this is something that they have to do together. Individuals cannot accomplish this by themselves or in isolation. It is the collective as a whole which is responsible for its decisions (and those responsible include individuals who

124

contribute to the process in a more indirect way). Fulfilling this collective responsibility is compatible with, and indeed depends upon, individuals taking responsibility for doing their share to make collective decision-making rational.

However, this account of responsibility is not going to satisfy many of those who insist that individuals should take responsibility for their own decisions and actions. There is more at stake than the issue of whether and when we can hold individuals responsible for what they do. Ethical collectivism, by objecting to the idea that moral rationality is complete within us, is in conflict not only with a common Christian idea that an individual must take sole responsibility for his or her ethical decisions – that she stands alone before the judgment of God as an individual soul – but also with the Kantian view that the moral law comes from within. Both place upon the individual's shoulders the entire responsibility for his or her ethical behaviour – the making of decisions as well as the actions themselves.[2] Both are fundamentally at odds with the idea of ethical decision-making advocated by ethical collectivism. From a Kantian point of view groups cannot make real moral decisions. Whatever a group might decide has to be assessed by the individual who draws her own authoritative conclusion about what is right.

This view of the responsibility of an ethical agent has had a profound influence even on those who do not regard themselves as Christians or Kantians. It is bound up with a widely held conception of individual integrity. The status of an individual as a moral arbiter or legislator is, according to the Kantian conception, what makes her deserving of respect. In determining and willing the universal moral law she is expressing her nature as a free and rational individual. Her identity and worth depend upon her having this capacity. According to the Christian tradition, the ability of the individual to judge for herself what is right or wrong, and act accordingly, is the basis of the relation between God and humanity and the drama of salvation. Given these influential ideas about moral agency, another rehearsal of the arguments against monology is not likely to be sufficient to shake the conviction of those who find it counter-intuitive, indeed offensive and demeaning, to place the ultimate responsibility for moral decision-making outside of the individual.

Ethical collectivism is one of the moral theories which denies the concept of agency inherent in Kantian and Christian ethics. It insists that we are entirely creatures of the empirical world whose outlook is the result of psychological characteristics, social relations and personal experiences. There is no such thing as a noumenal self or spiritual substance capable of rising above these influences and making a truly impartial, unconditioned act of reason or will. The denial of the metaphysics of the noumenal self is bound to have an effect on how we understand moral agency and morality itself. Ethical decisions, Bernard Williams says, should not be seen as something with a special status, requiring that individuals free themselves from the influences of character, sentiment and environment (Williams 1985: 65). Practical decision-making is influenced, as he says, by an ethical life shaped by others, by environmental circumstances, personal characteristics and goals.

Ethical collectivists are clearly not the only moral theorists to deny Kantian metaphysics and its related conception of agency. However, so long as theories of ethical decision-making continue to regard judgment as the province of the individual it is difficult to escape the influence of the Kantian picture of moral agency and the difficulties which go with it. For a conscientious individual has to recognise that influences of environment and character mean that her judgments do not have the universal authority which most moral philosophers continue to insist they must have. So if she is going to satisfy the requirements of ethical decision-making and make her judgment truly rational she has to transcend her particular empirical position and become the self which the Kantian model requires that she be. But this, as we have seen, is beyond her capacity – beyond the capacity of any empirical self. Thus the possibility of fulfilling the requirement that reason imposes on morality seems to depend upon a metaphysical view which we are supposed to have jettisoned. The metaphysics of the noumenal self is as much the result as the cause of the requirement of ethical rationality as it is monologically understood. How else but through a metaphysical act of faith can we make sense of, and underwrite the assumption that, the individual is capable of being an authoritative moral judge, the maker of the universal moral law?

Those moral theorists who deny Kantian metaphysics have not generally faced the consequences of doing so. Ethical collectivism makes a clean break with Kantian and Christian doctrines about the nature of the self by shifting some of the epistemological burden of ethical judgment from the individual to the collective. It requires us to adopt a different picture of how ethical decisions should be made: to focus on groups and regard them as the primary source of ethical decisions, to concentrate on making collective decision-making more rational rather than on trying to devise techniques for making individuals more impartial than they can be.

Ethical collectivism can be regarded as a plausible, if non-standard, way of developing Hegel's criticism of Kant. One of Hegel's main complaints is that the Kantian moral law, which is supposed to be derived from the rational will of the individual, is too abstract and underdetermined to be the basis for moral action. To decide what she should do, the moral individual will have to consult her own conscience. This means that judgments that are supposed to be rational and impartial really depend upon subjectivity and its caprices (Hegel 1977: 90–3). Hegel's solution is to ground morality in the ethical life of a community. In doing so, he does not intend to abandon Kant's universalism or the view that moral judgment should be rational. Since nothing is gained, as far as ethical rationality is concerned, by substituting the particular traditions of a community for the conscience of an individual, Hegel next has to determine what social relations and conditions make it possible for rational, free beings to lead good moral lives. This eventually leads him to the notorious view that a state of a certain kind is the supreme authority as far as ethical life is concerned. Ethical collectivism provides another, less objectionable, way of understanding the notion of 'ethical life' – but one that is truer to Hegel's dialectical critique of Kant than are cultural relativist or communitarian appropriations of Hegel.

However, the moral philosophers who have made a determined attempt to abandon the Kantian paradigm (and not merely Kant's metaphysics) have not adopted ethical collectivism or anything like it. They have generally moved in a very different direction. They reject the very idea of an impartial, impersonal moral law and argue for a conception of the ethical oriented around the particular needs, preoccupations, ideals and relationships of individuals. Their solution to the problems associated with impersonality and impartiality is to tie ethics more closely to the person.

Ethical authenticity

Some of the feminists who criticise the ideal of the impartial ethical agent also oppose the idea that ethics ought to strive for universality: for judgments and principles which every rational person can accept. Young's objections to impartiality seem to be objections against any attempt to rise above particularity. The ideal of impartiality, she says, 'seeks to reduce differences to unity'. It is an impossible ideal 'because the particularities of context and affiliation cannot and should not be removed from moral reasoning' (1990: 97). Attempts to achieve it always repress difference; they exclude those who do not think in the same way. Communicative ethics, in her view, should not aim for universal principles which everyone has to accept. It should allow every individual to express his or her needs and to work out what each must do in order to recognise and respect these needs.

Ethical collectivists, I have tried to show, agree with many of the criticisms which Young and other feminists make of mainstream ethical theory. They agree that there is no transcendent perspective or impartial reasoner and that ethical points of view are inevitably plural. They reject the dichotomy between reason and emotion, and acknowledge that moral reflection is different from scientific reasoning. On the other hand, ethical collectivists do not cease to think that discovering universal principles or guidelines is the aim of ethical discourse; nor do they abandon the ideal of impartiality. Young and others are therefore likely to accuse them of retaining a 'totalising urge', 'a drive to unity' which is incompatible with proper recognition of the feelings and commitments of individuals.

Young's criticism of generality is bound up with her rejection of the impartial, authoritative subject, and so it is not easy to determine exactly what criticisms she would mount against ethical collectivism. Nevertheless, there are two objections which those influenced by postmodernism might offer. The first is that the endorsement of a particular idea of rationality and ethical method creates a dichotomy between those who accept this idea of rationality and those who do not, and it marginalises those in the latter category. The second is that general rules, however arrived at, are abstractions which require individuals to turn their backs on their particular commitments and desires. 'Feelings, desires, and commitments do not cease to exist and motivate just because they have been excluded from the definition of moral reason. They lurk as inarticulate shadows, belying the claim to comprehensiveness of universalistic reason' (Young 1990: 103).

Ideas about rationality and method do indeed set up a distinction between judgments which satisfy its requirements and those that do not. But creating a dichotomy is not necessarily a bad thing. The critic must explain what is wrong with this particular distinction. It would be unfortunate if a distinction between those who accept certain ideas about rationality and those who do not were used as a justification for persecuting and belittling the latter, but there is no reason to think that ethical collectivism encourages such a thing. Ethical collectivism, first of all, is more inclusive than most ideas about ethical rationality. The fact that individuals end up with different ethical opinions, or that some reason in a utilitarian rather than a deontological way, etc., is not, from an ethical collectivist point of view, reason for thinking that they differ in their ethical rationality. Second, those who *are* excluded from discourse because they do not accept the ethical collectivist method are not thereby regarded as individuals who have no rights in political society or whose interests need not be heeded in deliberations about morality. Ethical collectivists are likely to agree with Young that dialogue with *all* individuals about their needs and interests is necessary for arriving at principled political agreements, as well as for making good moral judgments about how those who are not ethical collectivists should be regarded and treated.

The force of the second objection is diminished by the regard that ethical collectivism has for the particularity of judgment. The feelings, desires and commitments of individuals are not excluded from the definition of moral reason; constructive discourse takes into account the views of individuals in all their particularity. The conclusion reached is not an abstraction in the sense that it ignores differences among individuals or their views. It does, however, 'abstract' insights from the particular views of individuals in order to reach a general, impartial conclusion. This means that individuals are indeed forced to make a distinction between what they are inclined to believe and what their rational method endorses as true. All accounts of ethical reasoning force individuals to make such a distinction. The distinction takes a more extreme form in ethical collectivism because this theory *does* take differences among individuals seriously.

Young's criticisms of impartiality and universality could be understood as a protest against any attempt to abstract from or question the conscientious judgments of individuals. However, the 'drive to unity', the urge to find rules or principles that all can endorse, is difficult to resist. For those who think that ethical judgments can be rational, there are good reasons, as we have seen, for not wanting to treat ethical disagreement as a brute fact that we must learn to live with, and indeed Young's communicative ethics tacitly recognises the desirability of ethical consensus. In dialogue, she says, participants move from a consideration of their own needs to a recognition of the claims of others. 'On this interpretation, those claims are normatively valid which are generalisable in the sense that they can be recognised without violating the rights of others or subjecting them to domination' (Young 1990: 107). This seems to require that consensus be reached about what these rights are, as well as what to do in cases of conflicts of interests or rights.

These remarks are not likely to persuade those who are convinced that ethics should be re-centred around the needs, ideals and way of life of the individual and the community to which she belongs. Feminist critics of abstraction and impartiality are part of a movement in moral philosophy away from an ethics which takes as its central purpose the determination of principles, rules and judgments which every rational person should endorse. Proponents of this tendency are not merely criticising the pretensions of claims to impartiality; they want to re-define the nature and purpose of ethical inquiry.

Once we jettison the 'extravagant metaphysical luggage of the noumenal self', says Bernard Williams (1985: 65), we will recognise that ethical reasoning is not essentially different from other kinds of practical reasoning. In his view, the subject matter of ethics has been perverted in two main ways by the pretensions of the 'morality system' which we have inherited from Kant and like-minded moral philosophers. One of them is that it sets up a special moral realm with ultimate authority over everything that we do. When we abandon Kantian metaphysics and return ethics to ordinary life, he thinks, we need no longer regard the self, conceived as a moral legislator, to have the right of dominion. We do not have to suppose that morality must override our own interests and projects whenever a conflict arises (1985: 184). Another problem created by the 'morality system' is that its requirements are too abstract and impersonal. William's complaint is not merely that impartial morality requires individuals to do the impossible – free themselves from the influences of character, environment and sentiment. He believes that impartial morality is actually destructive of personality and ethical life. The Kantian idea of freedom leaves no room for individuality, and thus it belittles or undermines our own moral dispositions and impulses. Ethics, he thinks, should concern itself with how we as particular persons act in the world, and it should base itself on our dispositions and sentiments (1985: 191).

Charles Taylor (1989: 3) also objects to the abstractions of 'modern moral philosophy' and wants to reorient ethics around individuals, their needs and what gives meaning to their lives. The problem with impersonal or procedural approaches to morality, he thinks, is that they fail to connect with the sources of meaning in our lives which are capable of motivating moral actions, and thus cannot justify the belief that it is of incomparable importance to do what morality requires. Impersonal morality begets nihilism. A better account of moral motivation, he claims, has to bridge the gap between desire and duty, obliterating the distinction made by Kant and neo-Kantians between an individual's idea of the good, and what is right for her to do. The reorientation of ethics which Taylor argues for binds moral response to an individual's conception of what is supremely good: to the 'hypergood' that gives a meaning and coherence to her life (1989: 63–73). The moral judgments of an individual, in his opinion, cannot and should not be separated from her identity as a person – her good, her attachments to others, her participation in a community. Moral reasoning, he says, is intrinsically associated with a person's biographical narrative.

There are some notable differences between the positions of Williams and Taylor. Williams stresses that moral reasoning is simply a form of practical reasoning and does not necessarily take precedence over all other kinds of decision-making. Taylor, on the contrary, wants morality to have a dominant role in decision-making, and his primary reason for rejecting Kantian and other impersonal ethical theories is that they do not adequately underwrite the importance morality ought to have in a person's life. Williams insists that our moral responses depend upon our dispositions and feelings and thinks that rational reflection can be destructive of morality. Taylor's position seems to require that we engage in a considerable amount of reflection on what is supremely good and how our lives should be lived under the influence of this good. However, the similarities between them are more notable than the differences. Both are critical of impersonal ethics. Both think that the requirement of impartiality is an unjustified imposition on the individual – not simply because it is a requirement that she cannot fulfil, but because it undermines the true source of moral judgment and motivation. Both reject the idea that an individual is the maker or discoverer of the universal moral law and insist that ethical judgment has to be thought of as something done by real empirical individuals on the basis of their own feelings, dispositions, attachments and ideas of the good. Both want to alter our ideas about what it is to be a moral agent.

Ethical collectivism has a lot in common with this attempt to re-orient ethics. It too criticises the requirements imposed upon the individual by the Kantian picture of moral judgment. It acknowledges the cogency of an individual's own responses and point of view. However, ethical collectivism retains the idea that ethically rational individuals should strive to be impartial, that they should aim for universally acceptable judgments. It simply has a different view about how this should be done. So those who are attracted to the position of Williams or Taylor would be as opposed to ethical collectivism as they are to Kantianism, if not more so. For collective decision-making would seem to them to remove ethical reasoning even further from the feelings, judgments and identity of the individual.

What Taylor and Williams take to be the key issue in their dispute with proponents of impersonal ethics is the nature of moral motivation and its relation to the agent and her moral judgments. Both think that morality can only be rescued from nihilism, scepticism or the irrationality of excessive demands by rejecting requirements of impersonality and binding judgment to the ideals, attachments and existing motivations of individuals. Taylor, in particular, aims for the Hegelian ideal of a morality which bridges the gap between personal motivations and moral requirements. However, there are several reasons for being puzzled by the objection to externally imposed duties. The first is that it is simply not possible to overcome completely the gap between desires or objectives and moral duty. An individual's identity – her system of inclinations, habits, attitudes, ideals – is complex, and even an ethics built around her idea of the good is sometimes going to oppose itself to what she feels inclined to do. Second, it is not clear why we need to discover such a close link between ethical requirements and individual ideals and inclinations in order to defeat nihilism. Scanlon and Habermas, as we have seen, can give a plausible account of why individuals should be motivated to do the right – one that depends upon our arriving at a conclusion that others could endorse. According to this view, impersonality is an asset as a motivating force, not a liability.

The main bone of contention, it seems to me, is not how close reason is to will. Those who agree with Williams and Taylor have different views from the proponents of an impersonal ethics about *what* is morally motivating, and behind this difference is a disagreement about the nature of ethics, and the role it should play in human life. In Taylor's view an individual's hypergood should be the source of her moral motivation. Williams thinks that our reasons for action should have to do with our characteristics and relations to others. On the other hand, what is morally motivating for Scanlon, and for other supporters of impersonal ethics, are the conclusions that all can endorse. The ethics of Taylor and Williams is an 'ethics of authenticity'. Scanlon's idea of what motivates us presupposes the desirability of what could be called an ethics of co-operation.

An ethics of authenticity is inseparable from the search by an individual for a meaningful life and her attempt to discover and achieve something she can regard as valuable. This objective is the focus of her ethical reason, and the desire to achieve the good motivates her actions. An ethics of co-operation, on the other hand, is centrally concerned with how individuals with different values and desires ought to treat each other. Those who aim for an ethics of co-operation will naturally suppose that ethical requirements should be agreed to by all rational individuals (at least all those within a culture), and must be universalisable and impersonal. They will be motivated to act only according to the prescriptions which fulfil these conditions. However, consensus plays no essential role in an ethics of authenticity.

An ethics of authenticity need not focus on ideals which distinguish one individual from another. Taylor stresses that our identity as individuals includes our relations with others and our attachment to our community and its values, and Williams believes that an ethical life centrally includes relations with others. An ethics of co-operation can acknowledge and allow for the desire of individuals to live according to their own idea of the good. It can insist, for example, that individuals and communities should, generally, have the freedom to pursue their own ends. But for proponents of an ethics of authenticity, the search for appropriate terms of co-operation is subordinate to (if not incorporated into) the pursuit by individuals of their good, the good of their community, or the realisation of a moral character. And for proponents of an ethics of co-operation, the authority of universalisable, impartial requirements is bound to take precedence in an account of ethical reasoning and action.

What I am suggesting is that the real cause of the opposition between those who have taken different roads in their departure from the Kantian tradition is that some are inclined towards an ethics of authenticity and others, including ethical collectivists, want an ethics of co-operation. That is, some want to retain the Kantian idea that an individual who lives according to her moral will is being most truly herself; and some prefer to hang onto the claim that individuals should aim to arrive at a moral law (or at least guidelines) valid for all. The two are not completely incompatible. An individual can reasonably want to live her life in accordance with her values and also strive for consensus about matters of common concern. Nevertheless, the emphasis that Williams, Taylor, Young and others place on the former leads them to devalue and marginalise the ethics of co-operation, even to regard it as a subordinate or questionable enterprise. There is a tension, if not a downright contradiction, between the two conceptions of ethics, but it is difficult to find a non-question-begging reason for favouring one conception over the other.

Authenticity and its discontents

Some moral theorists embed impersonality into the very concept of a right moral judgment. Habermas thinks that the pragmatic presuppositions of language require us to justify our moral beliefs before others with the aim of reaching a universal consensus. His treatment of ethics presupposes that it is more like science than it is like the discourses he calls expressive: those in which individuals express their personal values or feelings. This is precisely what advocates of an ethics of authenticity are questioning.

Equally question-begging is the complaint against Williams and Taylor that ethics for them is merely a matter of subjective conviction, and is thus relativist. Williams cannot find any satisfactory foundation for an objective ethics, but nevertheless he thinks that the people of a time and place share an ethical life grounded on a way of life and the common responses that come from it, and this, he thinks, should suffice for an ethics which is simply another form of practical reasoning (1985: 110). Taylor thinks that ideas about the good are often shared by a community and that the ethical life of an individual involves having an identity with the people of her community (1989: 36). Advocates of the ethics of authenticity would probably agree that co-operation with individuals who cannot be persuaded to share the same good, or who have a different ethical life, is desirable. Nevertheless, they are likely to think of co-operation, and the attempt to reach a well-motivated agreement among such people, as merely a political objective, something outside the realm of ethics or marginal to it. To them, the ethics of co-operation is likely to be regarded as a political intrusion, a change of subject.

On the other hand, Taylor's and Williams' objections to impersonal ethics seem equally question-begging. For those who value an ethics of co-operation, the impersonality of an ethical proposition does not destroy its motivating force, and the kind of reflection that impersonality sometimes requires is not perverse. For those who want an ethics of co-operation impartial reasoning is a necessary antidote to bias and prejudice.

What these skirmishes show is that it is difficult to argue against a position which purports to define what ethics is really about. What seems central and important to one party is likely to be marginal or dubious to the other. Nevertheless, I think that there are difficulties internal to an ethics of authenticity which reduce its attractiveness (even if they fail to dispose of it).

One of the central ideas behind an ethics of authenticity is that there should be no gap between the agent, her deepest motivations and her conception of right and wrong. This seems to presuppose that an agent is, or should become, one with herself as far as her motivations and values are concerned. The conditions that agents have to fulfil in order to achieve this coherence in their lives and valuations is one of the principle themes of Taylor's idea of how we 'orient ourselves in moral space' (1989: 27). We are supposed to reflect on our moral responses and use them as a basis for the discovery and articulation of our deepest values. Our objective, or quest, is to discover what we can take to be the supreme good to which all of our other goods are subordinate, the good that gives a meaning to our lives. Our whole life and our moral actions can then be seen as a unity in relation to this 'hypergood'. We can respond to the world as moral beings and make well-motivated choices because our lives have this unified meaning.

Williams is not so inclined to engage in a moral psychological investigation of the source of our judgments. But he seems to assume that, for the most part, our moral perceptions and actions are unproblematically founded upon our dispositions, values and commitments. This idea seems to presuppose that these dispositions and values are coherent, that they do not generally give rise to inconsistent judgments, for otherwise we might be forced to engage in the kind of rational reflection which Williams thinks is destructive of morality.

Individual and social identity are not likely to be as coherent and unambiguous as the ethics of authenticity seems to require. Experience suggests that there are many individuals who do not, apparently, have well-integrated moral sentiments or a single idea of what is supremely good. Their ethical lives are influenced by a number of contrary dispositions; the values they share with their community lead to inconsistency in judgments. They do not have a settled interpretation of what their lives mean, and so their ethical judgments are influenced by a number of considerations, and they will sometimes be at a loss about how to resolve dilemmas or make their decisions consistent. Proponents of an ethics of authenticity are thus demanding that we become different from the way that many of us are.

How is this demand justified? If it is based upon a metaphysical belief in an individual essence – a self that has a pre-established identity, if only we could find it – then the ethics of authenticity is merely replacing one questionable metaphysical assumption with another. If it is an ethical demand, then it is even more problematic. First of all, because becoming a unified self requires that an individual distance herself from her existing judgments and the motivations that underlie them in order to reconcile or resolve inconsistencies in values, attitudes and dispositions. She must reason and reflect in a way that seems not unlike the reasoning required by an impersonal ethics. The relation between moral judgment, motivation and individual identity is thus not so natural and unforced as proponents of the ethics of authenticity assume. Second, the individual's struggle for consistency may actually amount to an impoverishment of her moral life and judgment if, to integrate her life around a conception of the good, she has to ignore or play down insights that come from roles, inclinations or experiences which do not fit into this conception of herself.

The ethics of authenticity also fails to resolve in a satisfactory way the tension between the inside and outside view of ethical judgment. The seriousness with which we are inclined to regard our ethical judgments when viewed from the inside seems to depend upon them being rationally grounded. If we are to retain our convictions, we cannot allow that they are beliefs which depend upon arbitrary attitudes or quirks of character. To satisfy our conception of what an ethical judgment should be, Williams supposes that moral convictions are grounded in an ethical life that we share with others – something that we are justified in taking more or less for granted. Taylor stresses that the hypergood which guides an individual's ethical life should not be conceived as an arbitrarily chosen personal end.

'We are moved by it seeing its point as something infinitely valuable. We experience our love for it as a well-founded love' (1989: 74).

However, a way of life or an idea of the good only looks inevitable and natural when viewed from the inside. When she looks at her ideals and judgments from the outside an individual can see that the ethical life she shares with others is just one way of living, and her good is a commitment which cannot be fully justified. Such reflections seem to undermine the power of an ethical life or an idea of the good to ground moral judgment and action. The force that seemed to come from an unquestionable authority now appears as a psychological propensity or an inclination towards cultural conformity.

How can an individual who subscribes to the ethics of authenticity retain her moral convictions in the face of a reflection on their contingency and limitations? Only, I think, by putting this reflection to one side and not allowing it to affect her ethical life. She must commit herself to living and acting in accordance with her idea of the good as if it were as well-founded as, from the inside, she feels it to be. She must refuse to acknowledge what she knows. In other words, she must live with a form of bad faith – not a good situation for someone who wants to be authentic.

The importance of being virtuous

We have a motive, if not an overwhelming reason, for continuing the search for an impersonal, impartial ethics. Nevertheless, this return to an ethics of right, especially in the form of ethical collectivism, could be criticised for ignoring one of the important insights of Taylor and Williams: that the ethical does not merely have to do with duty but with the living of a life, with character and its development. Williams argues that bringing ethics back into the context of a life makes it possible to question the primacy of moral duty. Individuals have projects and goals of their own which are integral to the living of a life, and ethical obligations have to find their proper place in this life. It should not be a requirement that whenever duty calls an individual has to drop all of her projects and activities in order to answer. In putting the emphasis on ethical life Williams is also distancing himself from ethics conceived as a system of obligations and re-introducing an idea of the ethical which gives a much greater role to the virtues. Both aspects of this account of ethical life seem to be at odds with the ethical collectivist position. If what a person does depends upon how she weighs the importance of her own projects against an ethical requirement, then it seems that what she should do must be up to her. No one else can authoritatively assess the value to an individual of her projects. And virtues, as they are usually treated, are personal characteristics, and therefore to the extent that ethical judgment is informed by the virtues, ethics is a matter for individual judgment.

One way of incorporating within an ethical collectivist framework the personal choices which are involved in living a life is to think of constructive discourse as supplying the obligations which a person has to take into account, but leaving it up to her what she should do with them: whether she should do her duty or pursue her projects at the expense of duty. However, this concession to personal choice is incompatible with an ethics of co-operation. For the importance to me of my project does not exempt me from having to justify my actions before others and accepting universal requirements properly arrived at. The choice between duty and the pursuit of a valued project is an *ethical* choice, and has to be treated accordingly. From the perspective of an ethics of co-operation the primacy of ethics is the consequence of how ethical judgments must be justified and not a questionable metaphysical assumption.

Ethical collectivism requires that individuals fulfil their ethical responsibilities, whatever these turn out to be, and it demands that in their reasoning they distance themselves from their own particular ethical impulses and perceptions. On the other hand, ethical collectivism relieves some of the burden of epistemological responsibility which other accounts of ethical rationality impose upon individuals. Monological accounts of rationality assign the task of getting things right to the individual reasoner. She can get help and advice from others, but in the end she is solely responsible for weighing all of the considerations and criticism she has collected and determining what is right. Every thoughtful person knows that it is impossible in many cases to carry out this task in a satisfactory way, and this contributes to the impression that being a moral individual is onerous and over-demanding. An ethical collectivist knows her limitations and does not think that she has to take the full weight of ethical decision-making on her shoulders. She also knows that the ethical insights which she contributes to ethical discourse arise from living her own life (as well as her reflections on the lives of others). She does not have to denigrate or push aside her own concerns and experiences in order to make a contribution to ethical reasoning.

The importance to individuals of their own lives, projects and ethical perceptions does not seem to be a reason for rejecting the ethical collectivist position. Neither is an ethics of virtue, properly conceived. Characteristics which have been labelled virtues are of two kinds. The first are person-defining virtues. The development and interpretation of these virtues depend on how an individual lives her life and learns from her experiences. They contribute to an individual's understanding of who she is and what it is to live a good life. They define or inform the perspective from which she judges and acts, and thus influence the moral decisions she makes. Like ideas of the good, these virtues are a form of commitment and a source of difference. Individuals are likely to have different ideas about what it is to be virtuous, or what standard virtues like courage or compassion mean and require – just as they have different ideas about what is good. From an ethical collectivist point of view, disagreements about what counts as virtuous are only to be expected. Individuals live different lives, interpret their experiences in different ways and have different commitments. There is no such thing as the virtuous man or woman who can authoritatively make judgments which others ought to accept. Nevertheless, a life lived according to an idea of virtue can be a source of moral insight, and constructive discourse will accommodate positions which arise from different conceptions of virtue or different ways of reconciling virtues.

Virtues of the second kind are goal-directed. They are characteristics that enable an individual to achieve a preconceived goal, whether personal or social. What counts as a virtue of this type and whether it should be cultivated by all individuals depends upon the value of the goal in question. The virtues that have greatest claim to universality are those which contribute to an individual's being a rational and sensitive ethical agent. All accounts of ethical decision-making regard it as desirable that individuals cultivate certain characteristics or have certain desires. Ethical collectivism, like other accounts of ethical reasoning, requires that judges be competent: that they should be rational, sensitive and open to criticism. It also requires that they cultivate the traits and attitudes which enable them to participate with others in critical and constructive discourse.

However, discourse is a collective procedure, and therefore an account of the virtues appropriate to it must include not merely characteristics possessed by individuals. The collective virtues required by ethical collectivism are truly collective. They are not merely characteristics which all individuals are supposed to acquire or even individual characteristics which can only be realised in appropriate group settings. The paradigm change I am advocating requires individuals to have a shared objective, and it also requires them to work together to ensure that the relations between them are conducive to the realisation of their objective. So an investigation of the implications of ethical collectivism for ethical agency should try to determine what collective or social virtues ethical rationality requires or encourages.

Ethics and society

Habermas and his colleague, Karl Otto Apel, have argued that discursive rationality makes far-reaching ethical demands on social life. To engage in communicative speech is to commit ourselves tacitly to the requirements of communication. These inescapable norms presuppose a speech situation in which differences of opinion on any subject can be satisfactorily resolved and the force of the better reasons will prevail. The 'ideal speech situation' was originally regarded by Habermas as more than a standard for discursive rationality (as I treated it in Chapter 2) but also for all social relationships. It was supposed to function as an ethical ideal against which we can measure actual social institutions and relationships.[3] Apel in a similar way converts requirements on discourse into transcendental ethical requirements.

> Human beings, as *linguistic beings* who must share *meaning and truth with fellow beings* in order to be able to think in a valid form, must at all times *anticipate counterfactually an ideal form of communication and hence of social interaction.*
>
> (Apel 1990: 47)

Ideally we should be free of all the social and personal obstacles which stand in the way of rational communication. We should be able to express ourselves fully and freely in relationships free from domination. Habermas and Apel admit that the qualities and relationships demanded by ideal communication are not fully realisable, but they insist that the normative presuppositions of communication can function as ideals towards which we should strive. They serve as a standard for measuring our progress towards a rational, free society. If their thesis is right, then anyone who accepts the goal of rationality is thereby committed to a substantial thesis about collective virtue.

Much of the criticism of Habermas and Apel's thesis concentrates on their pragmatic theory of the presuppositions of communication: on whether acts of communication can or do impose ethical requirements on us. But in the context of a discussion of the ethical implications of discourse theory the question of what (if anything) underpins the objective of rationality is not so important. We can believe, like Karl Popper, that being rational is a commitment which cannot itself be grounded (Popper 1962: 2, 231).[4] The important issue is what virtues, personal or collective, the goal of rationality requires of us.

There are in fact good empirical reasons for thinking that rationality is promoted by institutions that guarantee freedom and equality. Societies which put severe limitations on what individuals can say or do are not good environments for empirical and ethical inquiry. Unequal social relations limit participation in inquiry and discourse, and prejudice gets in the way of rational consideration of contributions. Nevertheless, the claim of Habermas, Apel and others that there is a *necessary* link between a commitment to rationality and a society which encourages free and equal social relations faces major difficulties.

The first is that an acknowledgment that social freedom and equality are likely to be good for rational inquiry does not justify the claim that such relations are empirically necessary conditions for critical rationality. A distinction needs to be made between the conditions that have to be satisfied if participants in inquiry are going to be able to acquire theories or principles which they have reason to believe are true and conditions which merely improve the ability of participants to do this. Forms of critical rationality – science, for example – manage to flourish in societies which are far from egalitarian and even in environments where freedom of speech is limited. If freedom or equality is not a necessary condition for being rational, then it would not be irrational for a person to value rationality and yet (because of her other objectives) not regard establishing free and equal institutions as a priority.

Ethical rationality, it might be argued, makes more compelling and extensive demands on collective life. For ethical reasoning is not something that can be confined to a privileged elite. Every person committed to rationality has an interest in being a competent ethical judge; every person has an interest in engaging in critical discussion with others about ethical matters whenever ethical issues arise. However, for monological accounts of ethical reasoning the connection between rationality and free or equal institutions is still less than a necessary one. Ethical inquiry would no doubt go better and the chances of reaching a satisfactory conclusion would be improved if free and equal individuals were able to engage in critical discourse with each other. But a well-situated individual in an autocratic or unequal society can reasonably suppose (according to monological requirements) that *she* is capable of obtaining well-justified ethical beliefs (on some matters, at least). She will acknowledge that her ethical investigations would go better if she were able to engage in open discussion, and may desire for ethical reasons that others enjoy the same favourable conditions for judgment. However, these considerations do not make the link between ethical rationality and free or equal social relationships into a necessary connection.

Ethical collectivism is in a much better position to claim that there is a necessary link between discovering and justifying ethical beliefs, and certain kinds of social relations. Having a complete set of cogent propositions is a necessary condition for obtaining ethical truth. Since it is likely that ethical insights which discourse needs to consider are going to come from marginalised or minority groups, an ethical collectivist has an interest in ensuring that individuals from these groups are able to become competent judges and are free to contribute to discourse in one way or another. Enabling others to contribute is, for an ethical collectivist, not merely a factor that makes discourse less prone to error, but something necessary for obtaining what we can believe to be true. So it seems that an ethical collectivist *must* value social conditions which enable others to contribute to discourse, as well as conditions which ensure that cogent views will be equally considered in discourse.

It would be tempting to conclude that ethical collectivism can achieve what a monological account of rationality cannot do: provide a convincing case for Habermas' and Apel's thesis about the necessary relation between rationality and a free and equal society. However, a serious problem remains. By pre-empting ethical decisions that are supposed to be made through discourse, the 'ethics of discourse' commits the logical impropriety I complained of in Chapter 4: it mixes up meta-ethical requirements with ethical prescriptions. The result in this case is that the ethics of discourse attempts to foreclose on issues which really ought to be the subject of debate. What freedom and equality mean, what makes these ideals desirable, how they should be related to each other, how they should be realised, and whether there are other ethical ideals which are of equal or greater importance, are matters which are supposed to be open to discussion. They are also issues about which people can reasonably disagree. It therefore seems mistaken to treat them as anything else but a topic for discourse.

More seriously, the logical impropriety Habermas and Apel commit, leads them to confuse requirements concerning the treatment of ethical positions with requirements concerning the treatment of persons.[5] In fact, ethical and rational prescriptions have different functions and different subject matters. Ethical propositions are about how individuals and communities ought to value and be valued, and how they ought to treat each other. The prescriptions that are entailed or supported by a commitment to rationality focus on how ethical *views* ought to be established, investigated and treated in discussion. Though a commitment to rationality requires us to be concerned about the competence of judges and their relationship in discourse, this is only because their characteristics and relationships affect the rationality of their judgments. As far as rational norms are concerned, individuals are nothing more than a conduit for ideas, criticisms and opinions. This means that, from a prescription about how points of view ought to be treated, nothing follows about how the individuals who have those views should be valued or treated as objects of ethical concern. It is not contradictory to insist that all cogent positions should be treated equally and at the same time hold that individuals are not of equal value. There is no contradiction in believing that participants in discourse ought to be able to put forward hypotheses and criticise those of others, and rejecting a political commitment to freedom of speech and action.

Those who want to be ethically rational, including ethical collectivists, are not committed by the requirements of rationality to any prescriptions about social or political relationships. Ethical collectivism can make no a priori pronouncements about relationships in society as a whole, and it does not provide a foundation for liberal, or any particular kind of, political morality. However, this does not mean that there is no relation between its view of ethical rationality and social or individual virtues. Every significant human activity encourages participants to adopt particular attitudes and values. A commitment to being a parent, having a particular career, being a friend, etc. encourages a person to develop his or her character and attitudes in a way conducive to performing the associated activities, and this development is likely to have an effect on her moral outlook. The connection between activity, character and moral point of view is not one of logical or causal necessity, but its existence is common and natural. Our activities mould our character and our character influences our moral point of view. The activities of ethical inquiry and participation in ethical decision-making are also going to be character forming, and thus it is reasonable to inquire what virtues and moral attitudes are likely to result from these activities.

Ethical collectivism requires us to reason collectively. A commitment to rationality is thus likely to encourage us to develop virtues and values conducive to successful co-operation. This means that when we reason about social affairs we will be inclined to favour institutions which promote co-operation. Ethical collectivism also requires that we appreciate and respect the moral points of view of others. It insists that a moral point of view is personal: that it is bound up with the life and experiences of the particular person who has it, and the attitudes and insights she has acquired as the result of living a life. Respecting a moral point of view thus requires us to appreciate and understand as best we can other people's ways of living, thinking and responding. It is difficult to imagine how we can do this, as a practical activity, without cultivating and encouraging in ourselves an attitude of respect for the individuals who have these ways of living and thinking. And so we will be predisposed to accept an ethical view which requires us to respect persons. A connection which cannot be established by logic may nevertheless have an irresistible psychological basis.

What respect for persons means as an ethical point of view will also be influenced by the attitudes towards individuals that discourse is likely to encourage. First of all, we can expect that those who adopt the ethical collectivist conception of ethical rationality would find it natural to respond with delight or awe to the creativity which individuals display in their ethical reasoning: to their potential for drawing out of themselves and their experiences ethical insights which others do not have. Second, ethical collectivists are likely to appreciate those characteristics of individuals which make them different from other individuals: their particular characters, virtues, attitudes, ways of living and thinking. For ethical collectivists these differences are not a problem; they are what make it possible for individuals to contribute to the collective search for truth. We would therefore expect ethical collectivists to favour social relations which allow individuals to live their lives as they see fit and display and express their differences.

The respect for persons which ethical collectivism would encourage is in some respects unlike that advocated by those influenced by Kant. Kantian respect is predicated on what individuals are supposed to have in common: namely, their autonomous rational will. Their other characteristics are either irrelevant to their status as persons or a hindrance to their ability to become what makes them worthy of respect. Such respect for persons is compatible with disrespect for the particular characteristics individuals possess and the lives they lead. Ethical collectivism encourages respect for individual differences. It inclines us to appreciate people for what they are and to recognise that their uniqueness, the ways that they differ from us, are themselves a reason for respecting them.

However, the most important result of adopting ethical collectivism would be the encouragement of the virtues of tolerance and humility. An ethical collectivist recognises that he or she is not in a position to lay down the moral law. She knows that her ethical insights do not reach as far as the truth. She knows that she is not justified in dismissing the views of others because they are not the same as her own, or trying to bully people into accepting what she feels is right. She knows that her ability to be a good moral judge essentially depends on others.

Kant said that there are two things worthy of admiration: the starry heavens above and the moral law within. The first is admirable because of its grandeur and infinity, the second because it is the product of a rational will that transcends the empirical limitations of the individual. Moral psychology has undermined the idea that our will and reason is anything other than empirical. An individual has no inner means of transcending his or her empirical limitations. Ethical collectivism provides another means of transcending individual limitations – by making the moral law the product of collective determination rather than the determination of any single will. In so doing it gives us another object of admiration: the collective rational potential of humanity as a whole.

NOTES

INTRODUCING ETHICAL COLLECTIVISM

1 This distinction is made by Philip Pettit (1982: 221). I have used his terminology.
2 It is difficult to be semantically neutral. Some philosophers believe that any use of the terms 'knowledge' or 'truth' bring with them realist assumptions. I agree with Alan H. Goldman's view (1988: 214) that ethical judgments that meet appropriate epistemological tests are properly described as true.
3 Works by these proponents include Amy Gutmann and Dennis Thompson (1990), Gutmann (1993), Iris Marion Young (1990), Seyla Benhabib (1990), Nancy Fraser (1986), Lynne Arnault (1989) and Margaret Walker (1991). The views of most of these are discussed in Chapter 2. Paul Lorenzen (1969) was the first, as far as I know, to advocate a discourse ethics.
4 T.M. Scanlon (1982: 110) argues that ethical motivation depends on an agent having reason to believe that he or she is acting according to a principle which no one can reasonably reject. John Rawls (1972: 17ff.) imagines agents to be in an original position making an agreement about the principles of justice that will govern their social relations. The views of these philosophers will be discussed further in the following chapters.

1 CAN ETHICS BE RATIONAL? THE PROBLEM OF DISAGREEMENT

1 Post-Kuhnian philosophers will point out that empirical reasoners with different paradigms may also disagree in their descriptions of even the most basic properties. However, the existence of a Kuhnian paradigm presupposes a kind of agreement that is usually not forthcoming in ethics. Moreover, Kuhn assumes that paradigmatic disagreements will eventually be resolved by the discovery that one paradigm deals with problematic cases better than the other (Kuhn 1962: 23–5).
2 Wolf's example (1992: 790), taken from Bernard Gert, is the question, 'Who's the best hitter in the major leagues?', which can elicit contrary answers, depending on what criterion individuals employ.
3 Wolf's example (1992: 792–3) is inspired by the film *Witness* in which a policeman trying to solve a violent crime encounters members of the Amish community who, as a consequence of their religious beliefs, are uncompromising pacifists.
4 What it means for people to have the same or different views about rational justification obviously needs further discussion. I provide this in Chapter 4.

5 DeCew is discussing the views of Stuart Hampshire (1983). She thinks that his insistence on ethical plurality and denial of ethical relativism are best understood in this way.

6 According to Brandt,

> What is morally right or obligatory for an agent to do is fixed by which moral system a fully rational person would support for his society in preference to any other or none, if he expected to live in it.
>
> (Brandt 1979: 306)

Brandt assumes that individuals do have moral motivations and associated feelings of guilt or obligation. The purpose of cognitive psychotherapy is to examine these motivations critically and to remove or alter any which are judged irrational. It should be said that Brandt dissociates himself from the ideal observer theory of Firth (225–8). He does not require that agents be impersonal or impartial. Nevertheless, those who have undergone cognitive psychotherapy are in the crucial sense 'ideal' agents.

7 Connie S. Rosati makes the point that

> in making difficult life choices, we do not face a problem that could be overcome simply by supplying missing information. Rather, we confront limitations that stem from what it is like to be a person and to have a perspective.
>
> (Rosati 1995: 299)

She is discussing Brandt's view of non-moral good, but some of her criticisms can also be applied to his related idea of moral good. See also J. David Velleman (1988).

8 Pollock (1985: 512ff.) has a similar idea about how to achieve impartiality. He directs us, when we are making moral judgments, to take away in our imagination features of the concrete case which connect it with us and our interests.

9 However, Nagel thinks that only *some* moral matters can and should be dealt with in this way.

10 Rawls is not presupposing a realist view of ethical properties. What he wants to demonstrate is that ethical generalisations can be objective in the sense that they are derived from a reasonable and reliable method. He warns us that 'there is no way of knowing ahead of time how to find and formulate reasonable [moral] principles. Indeed, we cannot even be certain that they exist, and it is well known that there are no mechanical methods of discovery' (1952: 178).

2 DISCOURSE ETHICS AND THE CRITIQUE OF MONOLOGY

1 In 'Discourse ethics' (1990: 49ff.) Habermas uses B.F. Strawson's account of moral phenomenology in 'Freedom and resentment' (1974) and S. Toulmin's analogy between empirical and moral reasoning in *Examination of the Place of Reason in Ethics* (1970: 125) to argue that our moral responses and the way we go about justifying them depend upon the presumption that ethical beliefs can and should be rational.

2 Rawls makes the point that

> A reasonable man exhibits a desire to consider questions with an open mind, and consequently, while he may already have an opinion on some issue, he is always willing to consider it in the light of further evidence and reasons which may be presented to him in discussion.
>
> (Rawls 1952: 179)

3 Susan Moller Okin in *Justice, Gender and the Family* (1989) claims that Rawls' theory doesn't take into account the systematic social disadvantage suffered by women and thinks that knowledge of this social fact should enter into decision-making in the original position. That is, she is arguing that the background information required by those in the original position needs to be changed. Making these changes, as she makes clear, is perfectly compatible with retaining the *method* used by Rawls for determining principles of justice.

4 However, Walker is not trying to defend Habermas' discourse ethics. Indeed, some of what she says is at odds with the advocacy of Kantian universalisability which is central to Habermas' position. Feminist objections to ethical generalisation are discussed in Chapter 3.

5 It is notable that David A.J. Richards (1971: 68) insists for similar reasons that those who make a decision behind the veil of ignorance should include all moral agents. He does not agree with Rawls that one person is entitled to make a decision on behalf of all, however rational that person may be.

6 Other political philosophers have related reasons for thinking it desirable for individuals who hold different ethical views to engage in discussion. Amy Gutmann and Dennis Thompson (1990: 88) think that such discussions not only encourage tolerance; they promote mutual respect (as well as holding out the possibility that some issues may be resolved). Iris Marion Young (1990: 92) suggests that a democracy which promotes discussion encourages citizens to think about their needs in relation to those of others and to take an active interest in their social institutions.

7 The positions of Habermas and Rawls are also similar to the 'path of conversational restraint' advocated by Bruce Ackerman (1989: 16ff.).

8 This view of the function of discourse ethics can be more appropriately attributed to Seyla Benhabib (1986: ch. 8).

3 THE NATURE OF MORAL JUDGMENT: A MORAL-PSYCHOLOGICAL INQUIRY

1 There is a hermeneutical view that self-understanding is achieved through reaching an understanding with others about what our verbal and other behaviour means. There is no pre-existing meaning for communication to reveal. For a defence of this position see Habermas (1971: chapters 7–8). My argument doesn't depend on the truth of this view: merely on what I take to be the common sense idea that we can manage to understand others.

2 It should be noted that Benhabib (1992) and Walker (1991) would probably not disagree with this point. They too think that there is a place in moral thinking for abstractions. My intention here is not to argue against their positions.

3 ' . . . I bear the responsibility for the choice which, in committing myself, also commits the whole of humanity' (Sartre 1975: 363). The account of moral judgment I give in this chapter is, I think, more true to Sartre's position than the decisionist view usually attributed to him. But I do not attempt to explain what he really means.

4 I argue for this in more detail in 'Moral difference and moral epistemology' (1994: 217).

5 Sartre describes him as being motivated by 'a sentiment somewhat primitive but generous' to avenge his older brother's death in the 1940 German offensive (1975: 354). This description suggests that his reasons for wanting to join the Free French would benefit from a critical examination.

4 REQUIREMENTS OF ETHICAL REASONING: CRITICAL DISCOURSE

1 Utilitarians are especially inclined to the view that they are redefining what ethical rationality means, and thus can ignore intuitions or views which are contrary to utilitarian judgments. J.J.C. Smart makes the suggestion in 'An outline of a system of utilitarian ethics' (173: 68) that a utilitarian might simply disregard any view contrary to utilitarianism because only the utilitarian principle is compatible with the general benevolence which ought to motivate all moral agents. However, he goes on to concede that this definitional approach is not an adequate response to the moral problems which particularly worry non-utilitarians.

2 Nevertheless, some moral philosophers object to the idea that ethics should concentrate on questions of right. I examine in Chapter 6 the views of some of those who think that our ethical reasoning should focus on questions about virtue or the good life.

3 Brandt sometimes claims that his cognitive psychotherapy can achieve this result (Brandt 1979: 126–9). My argument against the idea that choice of value can be wholly rational is similar to some of the criticisms of Brandt made by J. David Velleman (1988: 353).

4 It might be argued that there are rational reasons for thinking that some goods should be desired by everyone. Those goods which Rawls in *A Theory of Justice* calls 'primary goods' are obvious candidates, for these are 'things which it is supposed a rational man will want whatever else he wants' and he will prefer more of them rather than less (1973: 92). They include wealth, power and opportunities, rights and self-respect. Let us assume Rawls is right. However, these goods (with the possible exception of the last) are not for most people fundamental goods, but rather what they want as a means to their other ends. Individuals who choose to pursue power and wealth as an end in itself are making a non-rational commitment.

5 People are sometimes at a loss about how to make moral decisions and/or justify them. If so, the reason may sometimes be that their identity is not fully formed, that they have no clear way of perceiving. This is different from the situation described earlier of individuals who have more than one way of perceiving. Though I have interpreted the predicament of Sartre's student as an example of the second kind of situation, his case might instead be understood as a difficulty of the first kind.

6 If rationality requires that all individuals aim to be good ethical judges, then it follows that there are some value commitments that all individuals should make. I discuss this matter further in Chapter 6.

5 REQUIREMENTS OF ETHICAL REASONING: CONSTRUCTIVE DISCOURSE

1 Brian Ellis, my colleague at La Trobe University, made this suggestion about how the work of constructive discourse should be understood.
2 I argue in Chapter 1 that Wolf's attempt to argue that some ethical questions may have no single answer does not accord with the way we commonly think about our ethical views. Ethical diversity is not such a puzzling epistemological problem if it turns out that those who are in disagreement are not part of the same ethical discourse.

6 CONSCIENCE, AUTHENTICITY AND COLLECTIVE DECISION-MAKING

1 For example, Agnes Heller (1987: 240ff.) argues that a discourse ethics is 'etho-political'. A truly moral conviction is something an individual determines for herself by reflection.
2 I am not suggesting that either Christians or Kantians think that individuals should make these decisions in isolation without any exposure to criticism or any engagement with others. Nevertheless, Christian and Kantian views are inherently 'monological' in the sense that they insist that moral decision-making is up to the individual.
3 'In so far as we master the means for the construction of the ideal speech situation, we can conceive the ideas of truth, freedom and justice, which interpenetrate each other – although of course only as ideas' (Habermas 1970: 372).
4 Popper (1962: 2, 238) also maintains that there is a link between commitment to critical rationality and 'the recognition of the necessity of social institutions to protect freedom of criticism, freedom of thought, and thus the freedom of men'.
5 Recognition of this distinction may be behind Habermas' present view (1990: 85–6) that presuppositions of communication impose requirements only on participants in discourse – not on society as a whole.

BIBLIOGRAPHY

Ackerman, B. (1989) 'Why dialogue?', in *Journal of Philosophy*, 86, 1: 5–22.

Apel, K.O. (1990) 'Is the ethics of the ideal communication community a utopia? On the relationship between ethics, utopia and the critique of utopia', in S. Benhabib and F. Dallmayr (eds) *Communicative Ethics Controversy*, Cambridge, MA: MIT Press.

Arnault, L.S. (1989) 'The radical future of a classic moral theory', in A. Jaggar and S. Bondo (eds) *Gender/Body/Knowledge*, New Brunswick: Rutgers University Press.

Baier, K. (1958) *The Moral Point of View: A Rational Basis for Ethics*, Ithaca, NY and London: Cornell University Press.

Benhabib, S. (1992) 'The generalized and concrete other', in *Situating the Self*, Cambridge: Polity Press.

—— (1990) 'Communicative ethics and current controversies in practical philosophy', in S. Benhabib and F. Dallmayr (eds) *Communicative Ethics Controversy*, Cambridge, MA: MIT Press.

—— (1986) *Critique, Norm and Utopia: A Study of the Foundations of Critical Theory*, New York: Columbia University Press.

Benhabib, S. and Dallmayr, F. (eds) (1990) *Communicative Ethics Controversy*, Cambridge, MA: MIT Press.

Blum, L.A. (1988) 'Gilligan and Kohlberg: implications for moral theory', in *Ethics*, 98, 3: 472–91.

Brandt, R.B. (1979) *A Theory of the Good and the Right*, Oxford: Clarendon Press.

—— (1959) *Ethical Theory: The Problems of Normative and Critical Ethics*, Englewood Cliffs, NJ: Prentice-Hall.

Copp, D. and Zimmerman, D. (eds) (1984) *Morality, Reason and Truth: Essays on the Foundations of Ethics*, Totowa, NJ: Rowman & Allanheld.

Daniels, N. (1979) 'Wide reflective equilibrium and theory acceptance in ethics', in *Journal of Philosophy*, 76, 5: 256–283.

Darwall, S.L. (1983) *Impartial Reason*, Ithaca, NY: Cornell University Press.

DeCew, J. W. (1990) 'Moral conflicts and ethical relativism', in *Ethics*, 101, 1: 27–41.

Donagan, A. (1977) *The Theory of Morality*, Chicago, IL: University of Chicago.

Dworkin, R. (1977) 'Justice and rights', in *Taking Rights Seriously*, London: Duckworth.

Firth, R. (1952) 'Ethical absolutism and the ideal observer', in *Philosophy and Phenomenological Research*, 12, 3: 317–45.

Flanagan, O. (1991) *Varieties of Moral Personality: Ethics and Psychological Realism*, Cambridge, MA: Harvard University Press.

Fraser, N. (1986) 'Towards a discourse ethics of solidarity', in *Praxis International*, 5, 4: 425–29.

Gaita, R. (1991) *Good and Evil: An Absolute Conception*, London: Macmillan.

Gilligan, C. (1987) 'Moral orientation and moral development' in E. F. Kittay and D.T. Meyers (eds) *Women and Moral Theory*, Totowa, NJ: Rowman & Littlefield.

—— (1982) *In a Different Voice: Psychological Theory and Women's Development*, Cambridge, MA: Harvard University Press.

Goldman, A.H. (1988) *Moral Knowledge*, London: Routledge.

Gutmann, A. (1993) 'The challenge of multiculturalism in political ethics', in *Philosophy and Public Affairs*, 22, 3: 171–206.

Gutmann, A. and Thompson, D. (1990) 'Moral conflict and political consensus', in *Ethics*, 101, 1: 64–88.

Habermas, J. (1995) 'Reconciliation through the public use of reason: remarks on John Rawls' political liberalism', in *Journal of Philosophy*, 92, 3: 109–31.

—— (1993) 'Remarks on discourse ethics', in *Justification and Application: Remarks on Discourse Ethics*, Cambridge: Polity Press.

—— (1992) 'The unity of reason in the diversity of its voices', in *Postmetaphysical Thinking*, Cambridge: Polity Press.

—— (1990) 'Discourse ethics', in *Moral Consciousness and Communicative Action*, Boston, MA: MIT Press.

—— (1989–90) 'Justice and solidarity: on the discussion concerning stage 6', in *Philosophical Forum*, 21, 1/2: 32–52.

—— (1984) *A Theory of Communicative Action* I, Boston, MA: Beacon Press.

—— (1979) 'Historical materialism and the development of normative structures', in *Communication and the Evolution of Society*, Boston, MA: Beacon Press.

—— (1971) *Knowledge and Human Interests*, Boston, MA: Beacon Press.

—— (1970) 'Toward a theory of communicative competence', in *Inquiry*, 13: 360–75.

Hampshire, S. (1983) *Morality and Conflict*, Cambridge, MA: Harvard University Press.

Hare, R.M. (1981) *Moral Thinking: Its Levels, Method and Point*, Oxford: Clarendon Press.

—— (1963) *Freedom and Reason*, Oxford: Clarendon Press.

Harman, G. (1984) 'Is there a single true morality?' in D. Copp and D. Zimmerman (eds) *Morality, Reason and Truth: Essays on the Foundations of Ethics*, Totowa, NJ: Rowman & Allanheld.

Hegel, G.W.F. (1977) *Philosophy of Right*, in *Hegel's Philosophy of Right*, London: Oxford University Press.

Heller, A. (1987) *Beyond Justice*, London: Blackwell.

Jaggar, A. and Bondo, S. (eds) (1989) *Gender/Body/Knowledge*, New Brunswick: Rutgers University Press.

Janis, I.L. (1982) *Groupthink: Psychological Studies of Policy Decisions and Fiascos*, Boston, MA: Houghton Mifflin Company.

Kaufmann, W. (ed.) (1975) *Existentialism from Dostoevsky to Sartre*, Harmondsworth: Penguin.

Kittay, E.F. and Meyers, D.T. (eds) (1987) *Women and Moral Theory*, Totowa, NJ: Rowman & Littlefield.

Kuhn, T.S. (1962) *Structure of Scientific Revolutions*, Chicago, IL: University of Chicago Press.

Kupperman, J.J. (1983) *The Foundations of Morality*, London: Allen & Unwin.

Lennon, K. and Whitford, M. (eds) (1994) *Knowing the Difference: Feminist Perspectives in Epistemology*, London: Routledge.

Lorenzen, P. (1969) *Normative Logic and Ethics*, Mannheim: Bibliographisches Institut.

Nagel, T. (1987) 'Moral conflict and political legitimacy', in *Philosophy and Public Affairs*, 16, 3: 21–40.

Noddings, N. (1984) *Caring: A Feminine Approach to Ethics and Moral Education*, Berkeley, CA: University of California Press.

Nowell-Smith, P.H. (1954) *Ethics*, Harmondsworth: Penguin.

Okin, S.M. (1989) *Justice, Gender and the Family*, New York: Basic Books.

Parfit, D. (1984) *Reasons and Persons*, Oxford: Oxford University Press.

Parkinson, G.H.R. (1982) (ed.) *Marx and Marxism*, Cambridge: Cambridge University Press.

Pettit, P. (1982) 'Habermas on truth and justice', in G.H.R. Parkinson (ed.) *Marx and Marxism*, Cambridge: Cambridge University Press.

Pollock, J. (1985) 'A theory of moral reasoning', in *Ethics*, 96, 3: 506–23.

Popper, K. (1962) *The Open Society and its Enemies*, 2, New York: Harper & Row.

Rawls, J. (1996) *Political Liberalism*, New York: Columbia University Press.

—— (1995) 'Reply to Habermas', in *Journal of Philosophy*, 92, 3: 132–80.

—— (1973) *A Theory of Justice*, Oxford: Oxford University Press.

—— (1951) 'Outline of a decision procedure for ethics', in *Philosophical Review*, 60, 2: 177–97.

Richards, D.A.J. (1971) *A Theory of Reasons for Actions*, Oxford: Clarendon Press.

Rosati, C.S. (1995) 'Persons, perspectives, and full information accounts of the good', in *Ethics*, 105, 2: 296–325.

Sartre, J.-P. (1975), 'Existentialism is a humanism' in W. Kaufmann (ed.) *Existentialism from Dostoevsky to Sartre*, Harmondsworth: Penguin.

Scanlon, T.M. (1982) 'Contractualism and utilitarianism', in A. Sen and B. Williams (eds) *Utilitarianism and Beyond*, Cambridge: Cambridge University Press.

Sen, A. and Williams, B. (eds) (1982) *Utilitarianism and Beyond*, Cambridge: Cambridge University Press.

Smart, J.J.C. (1973) 'An outline of a system of utilitarian ethics', in J.J.C. Smart and B. Williams, *Utilitarianism, For and Against*, Princeton, NJ: Princeton University Press.

Strawson, B.F. (1974) 'Freedom and resentment', in *Freedom and Resentment, and Other Essays*, London: Methuen.

Sturgeon, N.L. (1984) 'Moral incompatibility', in D. Copp and D. Zimmerman (eds) *Morality, Reason and Truth: Essays on the Foundation of Ethics*, Totowa, NJ: Rowman & Allanheld.

Taylor, C. (1989) *Sources of the Self: The Making of the Modern Identity*, Cambridge: Cambridge University Press.

Thompson, J. (1994) 'Moral difference and moral epistemology', in K. Lennon and M. Whitford (eds) *Knowing the Difference: Feminist Perspectives in Epistemology*, London: Routledge.

Toulmin, S. (1970) *Examination of the Place of Reason in Ethics*, Cambridge: Cambridge University Press.

Velleman, J. D. (1988) 'Brandt's definition of "good"', in *Philosophical Review*, 97, 3: 353–71.

Walker, M.U. (1991) 'Partial consideration', in *Ethics*, 101, 4: 768–79.

Williams, B. (1985) *Ethics and the Limits of Philosophy*, London: Fontana.

—— (1981) 'Persons, character, and morality', in *Moral Luck*, New York: Cambridge University Press.

—— (1973) *Utilitarianism, For and Against*, Princeton: Princeton University Press.

Wilson, M. and Yeatman, A. (eds) (1995) *Justice and Identity: Antipodean Practices*, Wellington: Bridget Williams Books.

Wolf, S. (1992) 'Two levels of pluralism', in *Ethics*, 102, 4: 785–98.

Young, I.M. (1995) 'Communication and the other: beyond deliberative democracy', in M. Wilson and A. Yeatman (eds) *Justice and Identity: Antipodean Practices*, Wellington: Bridget Williams Books.

—— (1990) *Justice and the Politics of Difference*, Princeton, NJ: Princeton University Press.

INDEX